More Than Information: The Role of the Library Media Center in the Multimedia Classroom

By Lesley S. J. Farmer and Will Fowler

A Publication of THE BOOK REPORT & LIBRARY TALK
Professional Growth Series

Linworth Publishing, Inc.
Worthington, Ohio

Library of Congress Cataloging-in-Publication Data

Farmer, Lesley S. J.
    More than information: the role of the library media center in the multimedia classroom / by Lesley S. J. Farmer and Will Fowler.
        p.   cm. -- (Professional growth series)
    Includes bibliographical references (p.) and index.
    ISBN 0-938865-71-4 (perfect bind)
    1. School libraries--United States. 2. Libraries--United States--Special collections--Electronic information resources.
3. Instructional materials centers--United States. 4. Computer-assisted instruction--United States.   I. Fowler, Will, 1952-
II. Title. III. Series.
Z675.S3F2374   1999
027.8'0973--dc21   98-49575
                                                                                                            CIP

Published by Linworth Publishing, Inc.
480 East Wilson Bridge Road, Suite L
Worthington, Ohio 43085

Copyright©1999 by Linworth Publishing, Inc.

Series Information:
    From The Professional Growth Series

All right reserved. Reproduction of this book in whole or in part, without permission of the publisher, is prohibited except for not-for-profit educational use in the classroom, in the school library, in professional workshops sponsored by elementary and secondary schools, or other similar not-for-profit activities.

ISBN 0-938865-71-4

5 4 3 2

Table of Contents

DEDICATION V

ABOUT THE AUTHORS VII

ACKNOWLEDGEMENTS IX

CHAPTER 1: IT'S A DIGITAL WORLD 1
    Schools in the Digital World 2

CHAPTER 2: LIBRARIES OF THE PAST 5
    Once Upon a School Library 5
    New Vessels in Old Facilities 6
    Transition Time 6

CHAPTER 3: LEARNING SPACES OF THE FUTURE 9
    Linear Classrooms of the Past 9
    Enter the Computer 10
    The Creation of the Lab 11
    The Network Appears 11
    Impact on Education 12
    Non-Linear Classrooms 12
    Non-Linear Classroom Diagram 13
    Using Multiple Spaces 13
    Multimedia Room Layout 15
    Classroom Layout 16
    The Digital Harvest 17

CHAPTER 4: RESOURCES FOR LEARNING 19
    Media vs. Tools 19
    So Why Isn't Technology Incorporated as a Resource? 20
    Resources for Learning 21
    Managing Resources 22
    Engaged Learning 25
    High-Load Learning Curves 26
    Connect, Compute, Complete Recommendations 27
    Netscape Guidesheet 31
    Generic Protocol for Electronic Resources 32
    General Principles in Using slide Projectors 34

Table of Contents continued

CHAPTER 5:   **WHO SHALL LEAD?** 35
                   What is the World of the Student? 35
                   Partners for Learning 35
                   The Teacher's Role 36
                   The Library Media Teacher's Role 36
                   The Technology Specialist's Role 36
                   Interdependent Roles Task Table 37
                   The Fabric of an Educational Program 37
                   Assessment 40

CHAPTER 6:   **LITERACY IN THE DIGITAL WORLD** 41
                   What's Important? 41
                   New Indicators of Literacy 42
                   Media Literacy 43
                   Literacy Issues 44
                   Attribute/Teaching Strategy Chart 45
                   The Role of Technology in Literacy 46
                   Computer Literacy vs. Information Literacy 46

CHAPTER 7:   **PRESENTING** 49
                   What Do We Mean by "Instruction?" 49
                   The Student's View 51
                   Instruction for Student Literacy 52
                   How Can We Tell Students Are Learning? 52
                   Middle School Technology Sequence 54
                   Outcomes, Benchmarks, and Standards 58
                   Raising the Bar 60
                   Cycles of Inquiry 60
                   Technology Indicators (K-12) 61
                   Real Life Learning 62
                   Technology and Product Rubric 64

CHAPTER 8:   **MULTIMEDIA REPORTING** 65
                   Organizing the Project 65
                   Contract 66
                   The Cycle of Production 67
                   Use of Facilities 67
                   Project Calendar 68
                   Moments of Breakdown 68

Table of Contents continued

          Project Skills.. 70
          Completing the Cycle.. 70
          Electronic Portfolios... 71
          More Work for the Learning Team........................ 71
          Sample Equipment Program Report Form............... 73

CHAPTER 9:   **WHOSE WORK IS IT ANYWAY?**................................ 75
          Repurposing... 75
          Improvisation on a Theme.................................. 76
          Who Owns an Idea?... 77
          Is Code the Same as Atoms?............................... 78
          Tracking Ideas.. 78
          The Webliography.. 79
          Building on Student Foundations.......................... 79
          Redwood HS Library: Webliography to World Problems 1998...... 81

CHAPTER 10:   **WHERE ARE YOU IN THE LEARNING CURVE?**................ 83
          Micropockets of Technological Poverty..................... 83
          Adapting to Change.. 84
          Understanding Digits... 85
          Digital Push-ups.. 86

CHAPTER 11:   **LESSONS INCORPORATING TECHNOLOGY**..................... 89
          Lesson Key.. 89
          Lesson Template.. 91
          Mapping Rome... 92
          Exploring Islam... 94
          Castles and Cathedrals..................................... 96
          Freewheeling Vertices....................................... 98
          Supply and Demand.. 100
          Growing Up in Time.. 102
          Archetypal Videos... 104
          Morphing Artists... 106
          Safe Science... 108
          Water Survey.. 110
          Food on the Run.. 112
          More Idea Starters.. 114

BIBLIOGRAPHY.. 115

INDEX... 119

Dedication

To our families:
at home
at school
in our professions

About the Authors

Dr. Lesley S. J. Farmer is the Library Media Teacher at Redwood High School in Larkspur, California. She has worked in K-12 schools as well as college, government, special, and public libraries. Dr. Farmer has taught in graduate library school at the Virginia Commonwealth University, Villanova, and San Jose State University, and she has presented locally, nationally, and internationally. Most recently, Dr. Farmer received the Technology Award from the California School Library Association. She has written hundreds of articles and ten books on library science, education, and technology.

As an instructor with the Novato Unified School District in Novato, California, Will Fowler has worked with students from elementary grades through high school. In addition, he has taught the Technology in the Classroom course for the Extension Division of the University of California at Berkeley. He currently is an instructor with the Media and Communications Academy at San Marin High School in Novato and serves the district as Technology/Curriculum Specialist. He is co-author of the instructional book for students Adventures in Animation.

Acknowledgements

The authors wish to thank their colleagues in the Tamalpais Union High School and Novato Unified School Districts for their support and encouragement over the years.

Special thanks go to Don Zanini, principal of San Jose Middle School in Novato, and his wonderful staff with whom Will Fowler has spent ten exciting years developing the ideas in this book. Additional thanks go to San Marin Academy and to Tony Harris, who has shared many great ideas in inquiry-based education with Fowler.

Special appreciation goes to Linworth Publishing, which has supported educational technology and educators. In particular, Betty Hamilton's comments helped polish this work.

Most important, the authors wish to thank the hundreds of students who have worked with them over the years, proving the educational value of their ideas.

Chapter 1

It's a Digital World

Digital information storage has become a fact of life that must be understood if schools are to provide the education required by students preparing for life in the digital world. The slogans of digital life are everywhere, many of them becoming folklore for the twenty-first century:

"The sage on the stage has become the guide on the side."

"Roadkill on the Information Superhighway."

You hear these phrases at any conference on technology or media literacy. They underscore our bemusement in this time of transition as we seek to develop systems that will provide storage, access, and utility for the vast knowledge database of the planet. As we seek to become information managers, the data systems are evolving, changing, growing, and becoming more unmanageable. Facts and figures underscore this evolution. We are laying fiber optic cable in America at the speed of sound—roughly 720 miles of cable each hour. Web sites are being launched daily. Internet connectivity–the linking of networks–passed 200,000 interwoven networks in the late '90s and is growing at 100% per year (Dertouzos). Cable television promises hundreds of channels. The DVD disc promises to eclipse the storage capacity of the CD-ROM, which a year or two ago was considered amazing. Our entire nation—from agriculture and politics to medicine, law, and, most important, education—is affected in some way by the digital revolution.

The digital world alters what we know, how we know it, and what we can do with the knowledge. It has forever changed the way business is done around the world. It also has changed how school assignments must be given to children, and it has changed how they will demonstrate their knowledge to us. It has altered our perception of what students need to know. Is it necessary to teach facts—names, dates, places, formulae, algorithms—when these are available at the touch of a finger at a terminal, calculator, or personal communications device? Are we to continue to work exclusively in the world of text in a digital world that is bursting with imagery? These presently are difficult questions that are nearly impossible to answer. There is no time to complete the research that educators have traditionally relied upon to chart their course through changing times. By the time someone completes a longitudinal study, everything has changed.

What is clear, however, is that all information, regardless of its importance, is being converted into digital form. This conversion is like that which triggered the Renaissance, when handwritten manuscripts were converted to books with moveable type. Only now, all information—from formulae for genetic codes to *Richard III* and the *Mona Lisa*—is being transformed into ones and zeros and is being stored away on computer hard drives interlinked through computer networks. This means that everything we know on the planet may one day be reduced to a neutral information string, the value of which can only be determined by the viewer who decodes it. This is the future not only of print information but also of all forms of knowledge, whether it is manifested as text, graphics, or sound. Varying combinations of these are available in digital form for us to manipulate however we choose.

We don't even have a good name for what it is we are working with. *Multimedia* has become the de facto term for what it is that is supplanting many texts. While no one likes the word, we seem to be stuck with it for now since it at least recognizes that there are a plethora of media out there, even if one cannot name all the formats. This may be all to the good because media that are multiplying have been continually changing for the last 15 or 20 years, so an encompassing generic term works best. The term *multimedia* would be even more confusing if it weren't for the fact that the building blocks of information aren't familiar to us all. Multimedia combines words, pictures, and sounds. These, at least, are familiar. Yet multimedia has altered not only how we access words, pictures, and sounds but also how we navigate through their world and what we can do with these familiar icons, indexes, symbols, and emblems.

Most disturbing, multimedia works by treating all content as neutral strings of information. Reduced to code, content becomes a language where *The National Enquirer* is as complex as Shakespeare, and Marilyn Manson is as intricate as Beethoven. In *What Will Be*, a far-reaching book about the future of the information marketplace, Michael Dertouzos defines "Five Pillars of the Information Age":

▶ Numbers are used to represent all information.

▶ These numbers are expressed with 1s and 0s.

▶ Computers transform information by doing arithmetic on these numbers.

▶ Communications systems move information around by moving these numbers.

▶ Computers and communications systems combine to form computer networks—the basis of tomorrow's information infrastructures—which in turn are the basis of the Information Marketplace.

Dertouzos uses the term "information marketplace" to define a globally distributed system for the exchange of goods, services, and ideas that will be available to consumers in digital form. Educational systems are an important part of that information marketplace.

SCHOOLS IN THE DIGITAL WORLD

The reorganization of information into bits and bytes creates a new world in the school. The library of the past has now become the media center. The classroom no longer has rows of desks facing the chalkboard. New generations of computers appear every year and a half, posing an unthinkable inventory problem for audiovisual specialists used to dealing with overhead projectors, tape recorders, and VCRs. As the hardware changes, new software is developed to take advantages of the powerful new machines. The cut-and-paste digital world allows for rapid transfer of information, often without thought or honesty. The filters, which were once a guarantee of a safe learning environment for children, have been removed. Information delivery speed becomes essential. Media centers not equipped with the latest servers, high-speed connections, and fast processors are, in effect, depriving students of equal access to learning, which their more fortunate counterparts at other schools may enjoy. More than ever, the role of the school media specialist is becoming central to the process of educating children. As it becomes clear that there is more up-to-date information online than in textbooks, teachers and students will turn to the media specialist for help. School librarians, skilled in the mysteries of the Dewey Decimal Classification system must now be adept at the Boolean logic of the search engine. Unfortunately, they also must maintain their mastery of print media since books remain as important as ever.

As information technology grows, media specialists will exchange their supporting roles for stronger partnerships with classroom instructors. This redefinition of roles will require serious re-education of both classroom teachers and media specialists. This book is about the new role of the media specialist in the post-modern school and how specialists can take a proactive stance in redefining the job description. It is not about computer hardware or specific software programs; it is about the process of managing a digital environment.

Despite the explosive growth and dramatic change, certain observations about the current situation can be made. For example, with the exception of schools built in the last two or three years, the school media center is probably found in the old library space. Books may have been relocated to make room for computer terminals. The terminals themselves have been located in spaces determined primarily by access to electrical outlets, which may mean they are not in the best space for efficient use. In some cases, lack of adequate electricity in existing buildings necessitates total rewiring in classrooms and libraries. In some facilities, the terminals provide indexing for books and magazines, replacing, or at least supplementing, the old card catalogs. In more up-to-date facilities, the terminals are wired to the Internet. In some schools, they may even be part of a local area network that connects the entire school. Management of these systems varies, from tight local control by the specialist, to the ministrations of a school tech aide, to a district support team, which keeps the secrets of the system safe from the library media teacher, and are on call in case of trouble. But whoever controls the operating system, the library media teacher is ultimately the final arbiter of its use.

This is a full-time job. It comes in addition to of the full-time job the library media teacher has had as a librarian. While the new electronic cataloging hopefully has made inventory control of the books more efficient, supervision of the library and preservation of the collection, much of which is now irreplaceable, remains a major task. Aside from additional clerical help, there is not much to be done about this situation. The library media teacher has two choices: adopt a passive approach, and allow the computers to run themselves, which is a dangerous option, or learn the system thoroughly enough to maintain control and partner with the teaching staff in its use. This proactive approach is the most desirable.

How best can we achieve this approach? As a classroom teacher and a school library media teacher, we will share their thoughts with you. Where we have had successes, we will offer them, hoping that they may serve as models for your own success. Where we still have questions, we will ask them, knowing that with time and practice, the people who follow will discover the answers.

Chapter 2

Libraries of the Past

Anyone who loves books loves libraries. Those of us lucky enough to have grown up in the era when the Carnegie library was the cornerstone of a town or neighborhood's culture can recall the serenity of a trip to the library. The quiet pace, the librarian at work, the musty smell of books, the wooden reading tables and chairs, and the careful division of the books gave a sense of well being and order. It was an environment designed for people to effectively absorb information from print, designed for focus, awareness, and rumination. It was not a natural state for most Americans, and librarian jokes were the stock in trade of *Saturday Evening Post*-style cartoonists. In this well-ordered world, there was a simple progression of events, based upon the lending principle. Books were selected, checked out, returned, and reshelved.

❯ ONCE UPON A SCHOOL LIBRARY

The public school library was a different sort of place. At times it too bespoke the calm orderly perusal of print, but there were different functions as well. Students might come for a book talk or a story hour. At these times, the librarian—a specialist in print subjects for children or young adults—held court, and the students were taught to respect her and to pay close attention to the words that were spoken or read to them. Good librarians were helpmates with the teachers in promoting literacy and the love of reading in general.

The school library served as an information center as well. Frequently it was a hub of nervous activity as entire classes competed with each other for limited resources for research topics: the *National Geographic* magazine, the encyclopedia, or a selection of subject titles arranged by age group, which were safe and effective information tools for children. These resources were carefully selected and a large array of filters, from state education department lists to the ever-watchful eyes of parent groups, protected the children from inappropriate material.

In this world of print, the library was considered the cultural museum of the school as it archived the sage words of great writers and provided books for entertainment and selected information resources for children. Here the process was even simpler than that of the lending library. Students asked for "the right book," and the librarian told them where to find it or showed them how to find it in the card catalog.

In the library of the past, the job of the school librarian went beyond service to an important role as custodian of the collection. Books are expensive, and a collection is hard to build. Children are forgetful, often negligent, sometimes destructive little beings. While books are good for them, children are not always good for books. Protecting the collection requires a diligent guardian, willing to go the extra distance required to see to it that books are returned, damages repaired, fines assessed, and theft prevented. As budgets are cut and books become more valuable by necessity, the role of book warden becomes even more the focus of the school librarian. Increasingly, more and more books, which were once the mainstay of school libraries, pass out of print quickly, and good substitutes at reasonable cost are hard to find. Without them the somewhat arcane business of the curriculum cannot proceed. Spending money on expensive electronic data systems when the collection is shrinking and needs rebuilding does not resonate well with the guardians.

▶ NEW VESSELS IN OLD FACILITIES

Is there anything in particular wrong with this nostalgic vision? No, not if you only consider it from the inside. Inside this orderly world where information changes slowly, there is a wonderful balance and symmetry that could go on forever. Unfortunately, outside the walls, beyond the bookshelves, the digital information age has changed the needs of the customers who walk into this world. Youngsters in sneakers and expensive logo jackets, armed with the latest electronic toys and arriving at the doorstep on skateboards and roller blades, cannot be served by the monastic calm of the old school library. Here are students who must learn to sort fact from fiction as never before, arriving with such suddenness that the school system that has not kept pace may find itself in much the same situation as a society facing visitors from the future. If you are to serve them, you must catch up.

One unfortunate fact is that these "customers of the future" who demand up-to-date services frequently are vague about what these services are and how they should be used. There exists a large group of American high school students who are caught between the hype of the digital world, which they are exposed to through television, and poorly implemented school digital systems. For years these youngsters have been told that "computers are the educational wave of the future" and that "everyone needs computer skills for survival in the job market of the future." Students like these who walk into libraries of the past in their school environment are at once angry and relieved—angry that they don't have the latest equipment and relieved that they won't have to demonstrate its use.

▶ TRANSITION TIME

We are clearly in a period of transition. The passing of the school librarian as the warden of the book warehouse is actually cause for celebration as schools realize that students need professional guidance to help them evaluate and use a myriad of sources of information. Just as the teacher can no longer satisfy every student's educational needs, so too must the librarian work closely with others to provide a powerful learning environment for students. But the librarian must learn new methods. Gone is the permanent collection. Gone are the filters that provided certified materials and protected children. Gone are the familiar wooden card catalog and the date stamp on the end papers. In their place is the digital world of neutral information strings, available to children who can use a mouse and peck their way around the keyboard. As bandwidth expands, so will the amount of available information, along with an increasingly sophisticated media system of delivery.

Neutral information strings cannot be accepted at face value. Unfortunately, this is exactly what children, with their naive views and limited experience, are prone to do. Rather, information comes packaged with values, connotations, and biases. In the traditional library, a professional selection process "transparently" examined potential materials for their use and worthiness. This behind-the-scenes task may have been a tactical mistake since library users have never had to question the basic validity of available resources.

Typically, students learn how to organize a coherent world of understanding through professional guidance. This cannot be accomplished through the old system of limits and filters, which helped children focus by providing a selective group of targets. The information available is too vast. Limiting targets means limiting the breadth of a child's experience with the world, and that can be harmful, even dangerous, in the digital world. Children must be taught to think, analyze, compare, and prolong conclusions as they access the vast global database. Someone must be responsible for teaching information literacy to students who are barely literate as readers.

For this reason, school librarians must assume a more active role in the education of students. Clerical tasks must be delegated to clerical help. Student learning is the primary job of library teachers, and they must learn to foster such learning as partners with their peers in subject-area classrooms. It is a powerful role. Armed with an overview of the entire school curriculum, library media teachers frequently work with every student in the school. This is a crucial perspective to bring to a planning table. When this perspective is added to a complete understanding of the information resources available to the students and a knowledge of pitfalls to be avoided by students, this position becomes a strategic one in any school learning system—especially in the digital world. As the rise of digital systems alters the instructional strategies of the school, the supporting role of the librarian of the past becomes one of leadership for learning. This leadership offers broad-based communication and a strong variety of information literacy experiences for students.

Learning Spaces of the Future

As conversion to digital systems in the business world proceeds, we are observing many of the changes in systems that are dictated by the digital world. Corporations are restructured; middle management positions are eliminated; workplace relationships are altered; modular cubicles replace offices; e-mail replaces memos and conversations around the water cooler; and video conferencing replaces the business trip. This process has just begun, and many new business models are being pioneered. The workers for these businesses are being trained now in schools designed for the age of the factory. As the last steel mill closes in Bethlehem, Pennsylvania, and dozens of new information-based startup companies replace factories around the country, it is clear that schools will have to change. These changes will alter the structure of the school and the strategies with which teachers teach and students learn. They will alter the focus of the curriculum and, eventually, the curriculum itself.

▶ LINEAR CLASSROOMS OF THE PAST

The schoolroom has always been a world of straight lines. Enclosed in a box of four straight walls, with the furniture consisting of desks set in rows, the classroom was a world that led from the door to the desk and from the desk to the teacher. Behind the teacher was the great black rectangle of the chalkboard, the powerful information technology of the nineteenth century. Everything was arranged as tightly as a close-order drill and focused toward the teacher. Tall students sat in back; short, myopic, or disruptive students sat in the front. Anyone analyzing the structure of the classroom immediately would understand that everything was happening front and center. As a system for learning, this structure has been in place for centuries.

The design of this linear world was deliberate, supporting an equally linear curriculum dating back to the Romans. This curriculum was delivered by academics trained in their given discipline, experts who guided students through lessons as rigid as blueprints. Frequently, the goal of these lessons was not mastery of a topic but preparation for the next level of the discipline. Thus, students studied two-place multiplication to be ready for three-place multiplication. Arithmetic was designed to prepare students for pre-algebra, which led to algebra and beyond. Students learned sentence structure in order to complete paragraphs, and they learned paragraphing in order to prepare for five-paragraph essays. Everything was formularized. Class began by checking homework. This led to drill on the next concept and the assigning of new homework to be completed for the next day. Everyone had the same assignment; everyone was on the same page. It was an analog world—a world of continuous measurement like the hands on an old clock ticking off the minutes.

The system that evolved was direct and efficient. Lessons began with the teacher, who referred students to the textbook, which had been designed in carefully paced increments. The teacher supplemented the information in the textbook with lectures. If additional information was required, an occasional trip to the library was organized. During each unit of instruction, the teacher also drilled the students on the skills demanded by the discipline: problem sets in math, grammar drills and spelling lists in language arts, and so forth. To the student it looked like this:

Teacher
⬇
Textbook
⬇
Lecture
⬇
Drills
⬇
Library
⬇
Test

Success in the class was determined by the percentages achieved on the drills and correct responses on tests at the end of a unit.

▶ ENTER THE COMPUTER

Sometime around 1980, a digital device was introduced into this analog world. From the beginning, it caused trouble. There was no place to put it, so most teachers put it in the back of the room with the screen facing outward towards the teacher. This, of course, meant that one student at some point in the day would work with his back to the teacher. This in itself was a serious concern. For students, it meant that time spent at the computer drew them away from the lessons their peers were following. Inevitably, the digital computer put one student completely out of synch with the rest of the students. In the analog world, this is as serious as a scratch in the groove of a vinyl record—if it is deep enough, the needle cannot continue playing the track. Students who spent too much time at the computer fell behind their peers. Most teachers solved this by putting at the computer only those students who were well ahead or seriously behind the rest of the class. Or they developed elaborate partnering and rotation schemes so that everyone could get a turn, and they tried to work the computer into the regular linear mode of learning. Others shoved the computer into a corner or put it in a closet because they could find no value in a tool that did not support their linear box-like world. No one requested a second machine because it would only double the problems.

The computer was especially disruptive because pace was critical in the linear classroom, and to use an implement that automatically threw students off the pace was difficult. Staff development classes sprang up, and persist today, on "using the computer in the one-computer classroom." Most teachers decided that they could not use this new technology effectively without a better ratio of machines to students. Thus, the computer lab was born.

▶ THE CREATION OF THE LAB

There were several methods for creating computer labs. Less affluent schools pulled all the computers out of individual classrooms and grouped them together in a single facility. Other schools bought 20 or 30 new machines. Practice in these labs varied as well. Some stressed computer literacy and were taught by a computer teacher. These out-of-context solutions did little to change the linear classroom in the core subject areas. The skills taught in the computer lab could have little effect on general student learning unless, as sometimes occurred, the computer teacher worked closely with the classroom teachers on lessons they designed together. However, this was cumbersome and rare. As a result, for several years thousands of computers were introduced into public schools without making any significant impact on day-to-day student learning or the structure of the classroom. Technology was a separate subject and was taught in a linear fashion like geometry.

▶ THE NETWORK APPEARS

The sudden explosion of the World Wide Web (WWW) in 1995 significantly changed the view of the computer in the schools. But while the World Wide Web was a revelation to most Americans, for some educators it was only a natural progression from an existing system of electronic information services. The Internet had been around since the '60s. Universities had participated in networked research through such systems as ARPANET, which linked researchers for the purposes of sharing information and browsing archives. Public schools began penetrating these networks in the late 1980s with modem connections, and teacher preparation courses began teaching gopher searches and e-mail procedures. Most of these systems were slow and confined to the exchange of text. While not widespread, this created a cadre of classroom teachers and library media teachers who understood the coming digital information revolution.

With the introduction of the WWW's graphical information structure, the computer moved away from its role as "smart typewriter" and became instead a medium for learning in all subject areas. As schools became networked, computers began to appear in significant numbers in the school library.

Paralleling this shift was the introduction of simple multimedia authoring programs for students—programs such as Roger Wagner's *HyperStudio*, which allowed students to create hypermedia without learning extensive programming. The introduction of such software into the school lab made visits more appealing to regular classroom teachers and students, and labs began to be used less for computer literacy and more for core learning experiences.

At the same time, new pedagogical structures were developed—cooperative learning, team teaching, and project-based learning—all of which were supported by the digital world. Students captured information from CD-ROMs, laser discs, and videotapes. Investigating the World Wide Web, students reaped a rich harvest of text, graphics, sounds, and video clips. As a result, multimedia reports started replacing the five-paragraph essay as a method by which students could demonstrate their knowledge. Multimedia projects, which are best created by teams, require management strategies beyond the five-step lesson plan.

IMPACT ON EDUCATION

These strategies look different from the regular classroom. One teacher who had gained a reputation for excellence in teaching with digital technology was being evaluated for a mentor position. Students in his classroom were sitting in clusters. A chart on the wall identified tasks that were the responsibilities of each team—research, scripting, graphics, interface design, and sound. The teacher was walking from cluster to cluster, chatting, cajoling, discussing, encouraging, problem solving, when he noticed his evaluators leaving, with puzzled expressions. Catching up to them in the hall, he inquired if they had seen enough in their brief visit to form any opinions. Their reply: "We'll come back and watch sometime when you are teaching a lesson." After explaining that he was teaching a lesson—several valuable lessons in fact—and that on any given day things might look much the same or completely different, he convinced them to return and do their evaluation by observing his students, not him. In the non-linear classroom the focus rests on the students, and rightly so.

NON-LINEAR CLASSROOMS

Non-linear classrooms alter more then just the way teachers present their lessons. It changes the structure of the room, breaking up the straight lines of the rows of desks into clusters of desks or sometimes tables. Rather than discouraging conversation, this design encourages students to talk to each other. Students' eyes are not always on the teacher but on each other. During working sessions, students face in all directions, are free to move around, and set their own pace.

In such an environment, a computer is a helpful addition, available to students at all times for their own particular needs. Heavy demands are placed on it, however, since all the groups require it. Teachers working in this mode are frequently hardware hungry.

Such a structure completely alters the way students learn. Instead of depending upon a teacher for direction, students learn to direct their own learning. In the digital world, the textbook is just a starting point. If it is used at all, it is merely to establish a baseline of knowledge from which students can generate questions for research and analysis. From there students turn to digital tools for information. If they have the expertise, teachers may continue to lecture and to offer skills drills in each discipline. They continue to assess students' progress, but now assessment is embedded throughout the process rather than at the end of a lesson. Assessment is much more varied and depends on rubrics tied to performance standards rather than simple percentages. Students play a role in the creation of these rubrics and understand their rationale. Such a structure is hard to chart since it mimics the digital world. Starting points grow out of previous knowledge, and progress tends to spiral rather than follow straight lines. A diagram might look like the one on page thirteen (beginning at the top and working down to "publication"):

USING MULTIPLE SPACES

Such a dynamic structure cannot be contained within the walls of a single classroom. The information flow reaches outside the classroom and requires students to follow its path. Teachers must learn to use learning spaces throughout the school, beginning with their classroom and extending to the school computer lab and the library media center.

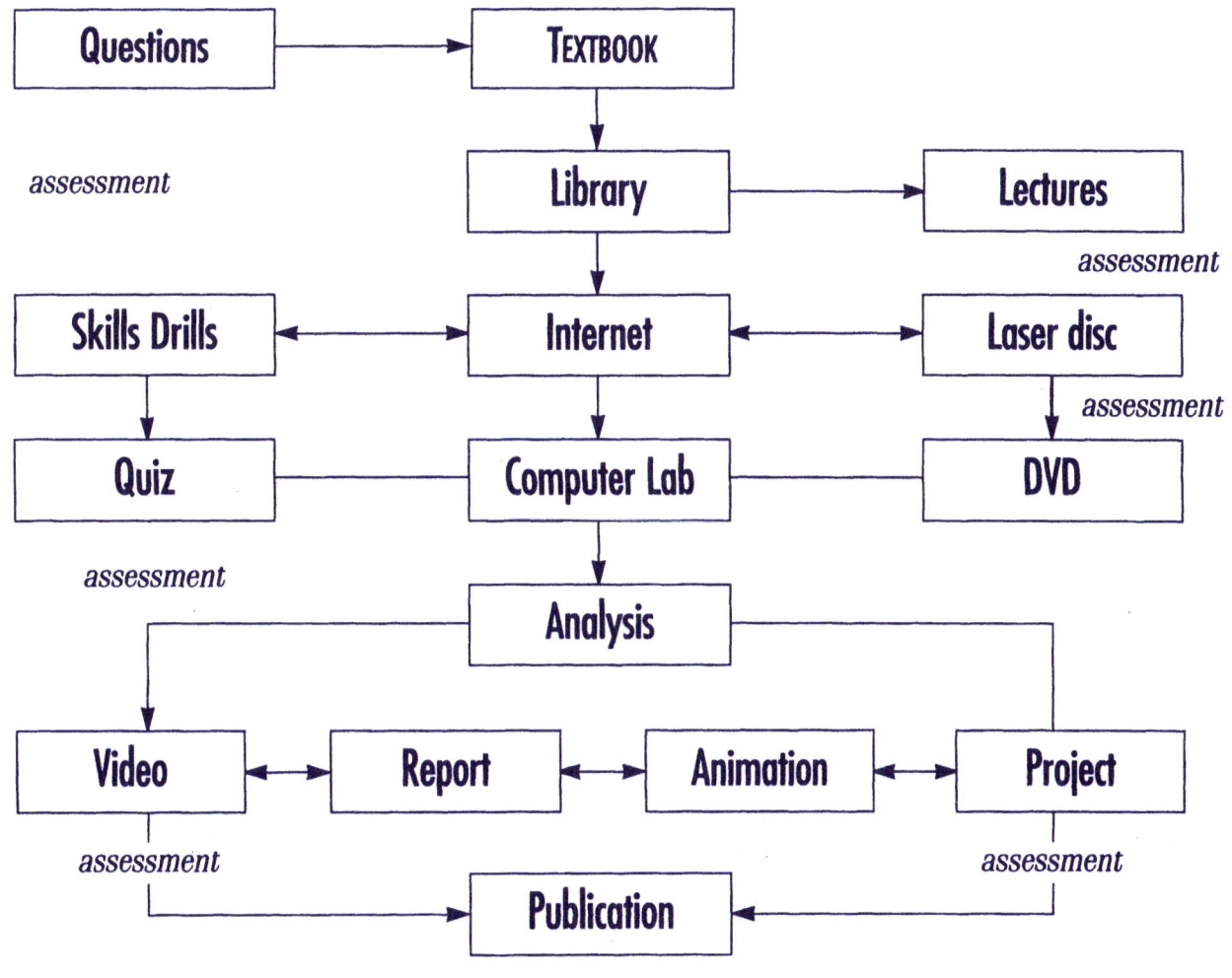

Only by balancing these spaces and maximizing the potential of each can a teacher hope to provide an adequate program for students of the digital world. Fortunately, the plasticity of digital media helps the teacher organize information in a variety of meaningful ways. With a little thought, the teacher can organize a schedule in which the learning follows a cycle that brings information from outside the walls into the students' workspace.

The teacher must begin by first recognizing the spaces where learning occurs. Learning begins in the classroom, to be sure, where topics are defined, projects are designed, and assessment occurs. But, in the future, most classrooms will be connected directly to homes through wide area networks (WANs). We already have students who work on projects in the classroom, "zip" their files with compression technology, and e-mail them back and forth from school to home in order to do their homework. Soon this will be the norm at any reasonably equipped school. As teachers begin to grasp the power of network technology, we can expect school servers to act as repositories of student electronic portfolios, which students may update from their homes. Therefore, more than ever the home will be an equal partner with the classroom. This transformation is already underway at the university level, where large sections of coursework are now online, and students do their research electronically from their dorm rooms and e-mail the results to professors. The efficiency of such systems is already available in some K-12 environments.

Because these systems of learning require that all students have access to computers, the school computer lab becomes more important than ever. All teachers must become familiar with the software necessary for success in their discipline and must understand how to introduce it to their students so that they can use it effectively. Fortunately, most good software is designed to be learned intuitively, and students have little difficulty learning to operate it after an initial period of introduction. In the computer lab, students take the ideas they have developed in the classroom and at home and build representations of their knowledge, from word-processed documents to sophisticated multimedia presentations. Visualization software, including animation and 3D modeling becomes important, as students move away from a pure text environment. Sound, from music to narration, is manipulated to help students demonstrate a point. Video clips are incorporated into the final product. The availability of these media ensures that different modalities of learning are accommodated.

The computer lab must not be an isolated space. It needs to be a part of the school local area network (LAN), so that work in one space can be transferred to other workspaces. The work done in the computer lab also must directly support the work of the classroom—computer enrichment activities that offer exercises to demonstrate mechanical agility will not provide the acceleration of content-based learning of which the computer is capable. In addition to operating on the local area network, the computer lab must be linked to the wide area network, so students may go beyond the walls—where the real information resides.

Thus we have developed three physical learning spaces—the classroom, the home, and the computer lab—which are linked together and are of equal importance to the students. The fourth space within the school that the teacher must be able to use is the library media center. Efficient use of this facility is crucial. Ideally, the library media center is the information control center, with a range of digital tools available to students, and access to rich information sources both in print and digital format. In addition, the facility has enough terminals linked to the Internet for efficient student access. Once students have formulated questions with their teacher, a trip to the information center is the obvious next step. But although it seems obvious, it is sometimes overlooked by teachers who are more interested in getting students into the computer lab to work. Even teachers who understand the value of the library media center may fail to coordinate their visit to the facility with the library media teacher, thus losing precious time and making ineffective use of the resources there. In an effective inquiry-based lesson, the library media teacher has been involved in the planning from the start and has pre-marked the various resources that students will need. Such assistance is invaluable, and most teachers will quickly learn to take advantage of this teamwork.

In addition to physical learning spaces, there exist virtual learning spaces via the Internet where students may interact with peers or experts through e-mail or videoconference systems. Many experts believe that these virtual learning spaces will eclipse the physical learning environments in the near future.

MULTIMEDIA ROOM

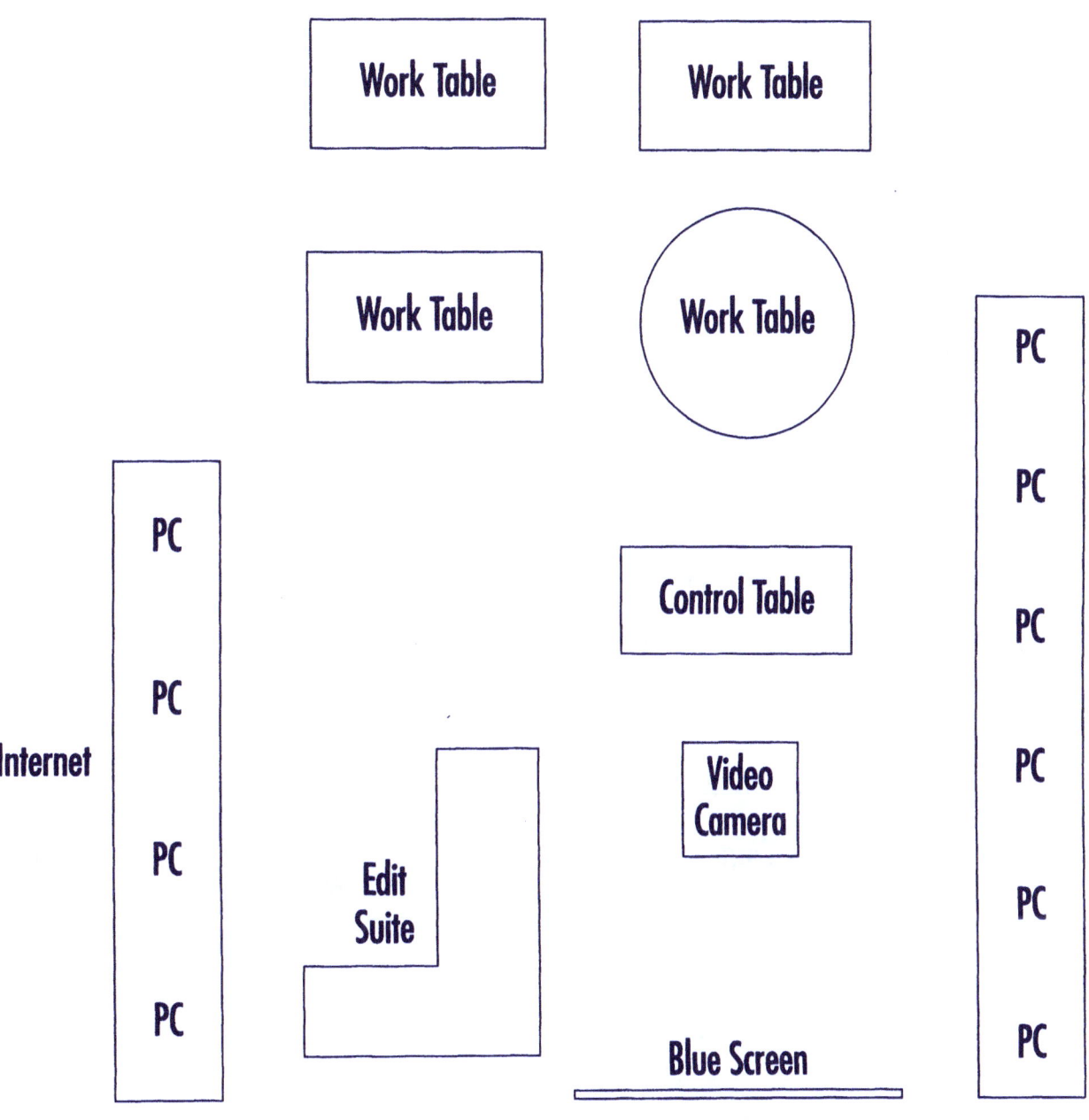

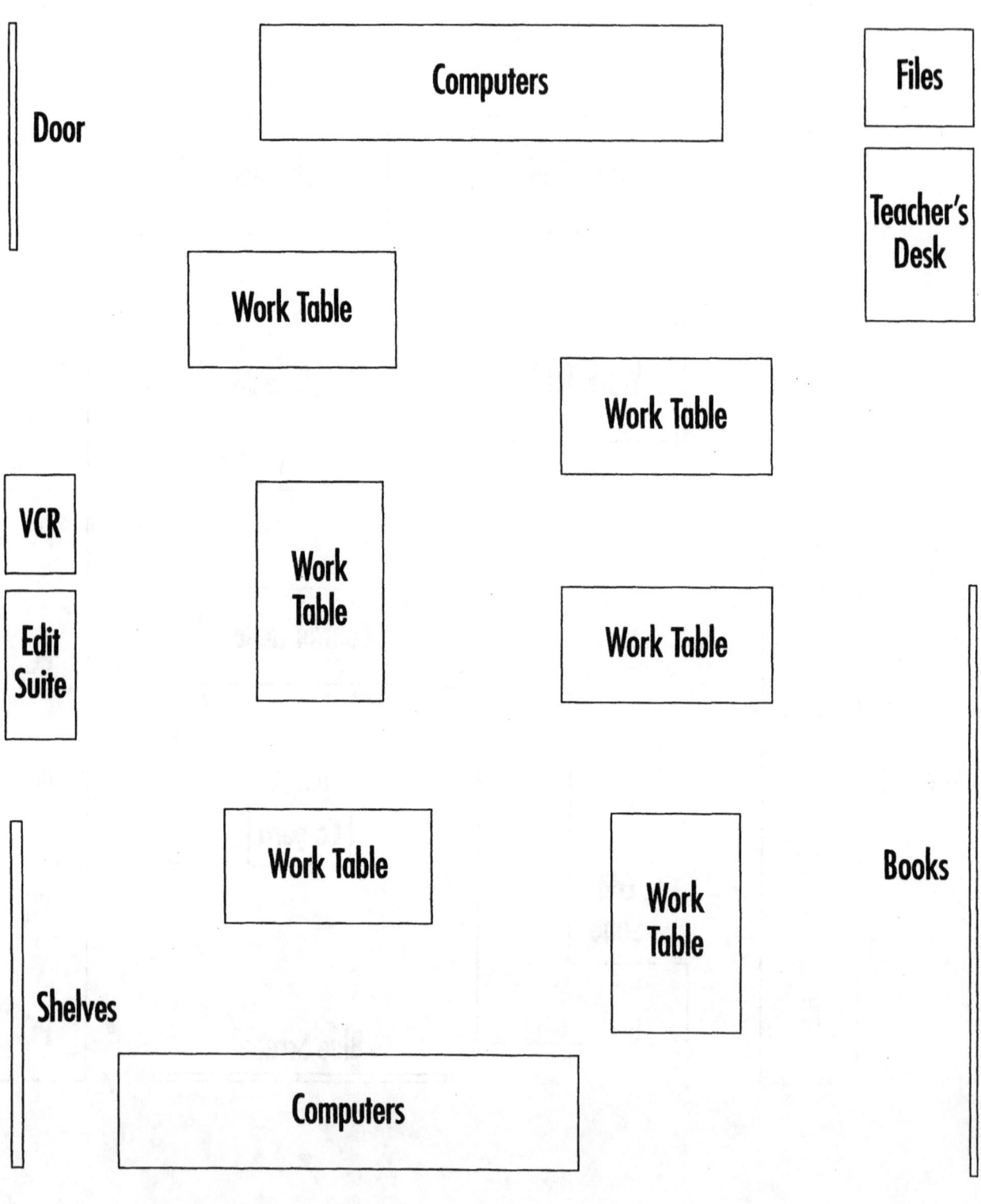

THE DIGITAL HARVEST

Students doing work in the digital world harvest an interesting collection of data. Where once most school research was text-oriented, now students can collect text, imagery, sounds, video clips, and other hypermedia—all in digital format. The teacher who sends students to the library media center without data disks is starting off poorly. There is no need for students to physically write or key text off the screens. They simply highlight, copy and paste the information they find into their own documents. They can include imagery or sound as well. The ease with which this can be done catches some teachers off guard and frightens others, raising the specter of plagiarism. For the present, however, the first issue for teachers needs to be this: Once students get their hands on all this information, how do they make use of it?

Essentially, the term "classroom of the future" really means the classroom that will exist whenever a given school gets around to implementing the lessons of the present digital world. Such classrooms currently require three or more learning spaces in the school since hardware needs to be time-shared. These classrooms may involve two or three professionals who work with the individual classroom "sets" of students. Some of these professionals also are time-shared by the entire school. Students help dictate the pace of learning and the scope of coverage on a given topic. Teachers learn to manage schedules and agendas for various configurations of students, from individual learners to teams. And they learn that it is important not to work in isolation, but to involve the library media teacher and the school technical resource people before, during, and after each lesson. They learn to see lesson design as a process, with multiple outcomes and assessments. As we complete the installation of the necessary hardware nationwide, more and more schools are ready to become classrooms of the future. We are just waiting to flip the switch.

Resources for Learning

It has been said that teachers teach students, not subjects. But since the main goal is to prepare young people to become lifelong learners and contributing citizens, subject matter is important. The educational question becomes: "What contributes to effective learning?" The answer is a stimulating environment where students can interact on a personal and meaningful basis with information and ideas. Thus, the wise development and deployment of resources becomes a central task for library media and classroom teachers.

➤ MEDIA VS TOOLS

It used to be simple. In the past, the educational system was one in which students retrieved thought from paper sources, manipulated this thought according to teacher instruction, and returned the thought back onto paper so the teacher could assess the manipulation. This was true whether students copied problem sets from math books onto binder paper, answered questions at the end of a science or social studies text chapter, or diagrammed sentences in English class. The typical cycle was paper to thought and back to paper. The tools of the educational trade were centuries old: manuscript and writing implements.

In the digital age, the educational tools have changed dramatically. Students access information from screens, often working with imagery as much as text. Increasingly more information is provided through sound or video so that auditory sources of thought are becoming ubiquitous. In fact, much of the thought from these screens is manipulated without ever using paper.

Moreover, media jump starts student attention. In neural psychology, the impact of attention cannot be denied. The synapses of the brain's neurons are not activated until the brain itself is somehow attuned to the stimulus at hand. Once that initial spark is ignited, the connections can be made. The implication for media and education is that visual or motion media may interest a student more than the black-and-white pages of a book. When that student becomes engaged, the brain also becomes engaged and is open to learn.

Since there are many forms of media from which to choose and education is, quite frankly, in competition with these societal messages, educators need to employ high-quality, high-content media in their instruction. The ultimate questions are: "What is the most effective way to communicate information?" and "What will engage student learning?" For example, what is the most effective way to communicate about the contributions of Martin Luther King, Jr.? Probably a combination of video (his speeches), print (his essays and newspaper articles), and photos (his prison stay and other civil rights events). The main consideration is to involve all the senses, emotions, and intellect of the student in reference to the content material.

Another feature of these new resources is the ability to tailor them to the individual needs of a given student. These mass-production techniques of the workbook and ditto are giving way to the selection of materials that are useful at the learning threshold of each student. This ability to customize materials for individuals may be the true revolution that the digital world will create. More students are selecting the materials with which they will learn—either through the Internet or other media channels.

One should note that tools are necessary in the educational world because of their use in presenting information—that is, student products. Just as educators have to decide what resources in what media best communicate information, students now have to determine how to share their findings. Sometimes teachers make that decision because they want to structure the students' learning environment so they will concentrate on the content rather than the media. A teacher may decide that the best way for students to demonstrate their learning about the atomic bomb is to deliver a debate on the subject. For a culminating project on a presidential campaign, a hypermedia stack or videotape would work. The critical piece is determining the attributes of the concept and matching it with the attributes of the medium under consideration. In some cases, the teacher makes the decision, but as students become more aware of the characteristics of media, they can decide on the media to use to share their newfound knowledge.

➤ SO WHY ISN'T TECHNOLOGY INCORPORATED AS A RESOURCE?

There are several reasons why new technologies have not been as successful in the school environment as they have been in business, and most of these reasons have little to do with the viability of the technologies themselves. The first reason is connectivity. Few schools have completed the necessary infrastructure required to allow all students, or even all teachers, to work with electronic tools during the bulk of their workday. It is inconceivable that a stockbroker would work without a computer and a high-speed data line at his desk or that systems design engineers would have access to a computer once a week in a lab where they would have to share that system. While we can never expect schools to own the tools that businesses take for granted, there should be a sufficient level of infrastructure within schools for students to use technology appropriately.

The second reason for technology's lack of impact on programs is training—both of teachers, who must understand the uses of technology, and students, who must use it to their benefit. Training is a two-fold process. Users must understand not only how to run the hardware and control the software but also how best to apply tools to the curriculum. We are still at the first level of computer training in most school districts. We are learning what a computer is and what it can do, not how it can become an integral part of the learning environment.

The third reason for the failure of technology in schools is resistance—from funding agencies to the expense involved, from site administrators to the need for training, and from teachers to implementing the new teaching strategies which technology requires. It is easy to rail against teachers since they are the ultimate gatekeepers of reform in the schools. However, given the level of support they receive, it is easy to understand their position. Most teachers have had technology thrust upon them without any assistance or training. For many teachers, being told "You will teacher with computers this year" is nearly as bad as being told "You will teach in Chinese this year—and we will give you two workshops this summer to prepare you."

Despite the less than impressive record of the first 20 years of computers in the schools, it is easy to be confident about the future. Much has been learned during the early years of trial and error. The need for funding is now apparent. The California government, for one, is now willing to spend millions to help its students "compute and compete." Infrastructure development has improved dramatically since the development of the World Wide Web. Businesses dependent on technology need workers who are trained in those skills related to its use, and they are partnering with education to help close gaps through such means as training systems for teachers. A new, youthful workforce is entering the teaching profession, and resistant veteran teachers are learning the power of technology for education. As these developments multiply, the focus should get away from the machine and back to learning.

▷ RESOURCES FOR LEARNING

No one textbook can address all of the informational needs of all students. The reading level alone can be either too simplistic or too challenging for students in a classroom. The limitations of print also constrain student learning. The school library media center has stood as the institutional center of information because of its collection of relevant resources. Even in the traditional library, print material is available on a variety of reading levels and perspectives. Some books were text-heavy while other focused on illustrative examples. The role of the librarian has been to match the resource with the student.

Presently, the library's collection of resources has the potential of embracing a number of media. Here are some of the possibilities:

▶ Audiocassettes: for speeches, oral histories, and environmental "flavorings"

▶ Videotapes: for recording movement and time-sensitive documents

▶ Photographs: for documenting events and people

▶ Slides: for high-resolution visuals, particularly sequenced for presentations

▶ CDs: for documenting music and speeches

▶ CD-ROMs and laser discs: for random access to text, graphics, movement, and sound

▶ Multimedia documents: for exploring content in a variety of ways (both in terms of access and content format)

▶ Internet: for a wide range of media sources from around the world.

Regardless of medium, the criteria for resource selection is still to support and supplement the school's curriculum. Content still needs to be accurate and provide a balanced perspective. Technical aspects have changed; library media teachers need to consider the format's physical quality and delivery. Is the sound clear, and is the picture quality focused? Does the narration fit the imagery, and are navigational tools user-friendly?

Library media teachers (LMTs) also must understand the full range of interests and abilities that students possess, and they need to develop collections that address those factors. This task adds more responsibility for educators, who select these materials and guide their constituents in selecting appropriate resources. While this is an opportunity to accommodate the diversity of the American school population, it is a tremendous challenge that requires a skilled curriculum specialist.

A major resource selection issue facing LMTs is the Internet. When the resources are located within the library media center, control is simple. Even with interlibrary loan, the LMT determined which materials to borrow. But the Internet is definitely outside the LMT's sphere of influence. Sources are "housed" throughout the world, and quality control varies tremendously. At best, the LMT may bookmark high-quality resources or develop navigational tools to guide students to selected materials. On a deeper level, the LMT has to share the selection task with the entire school, explaining how to assess resources and make individual access decisions. For some LMTs, the thought of such wide-based training seems to "de-professionalize" the process. However, it can actually make people more aware of the difficult task of selection and encourage them to partner more frequently with the LMT.

In response to this growing issue, there has been some effort toward assisting site personnel with resource deployment. Some of this effort is a natural outgrowth of the burgeoning Internet, which has required professional search engines and indexing systems for navigational ideas. Professionals have begun to set up clearinghouses for educators, which pull together online resource by curriculum area. An example of this direction is SCORE (Schools in California Online Resources for Education), a set of Web-based lists maintained through the California Department of Education. As these online resources and indexed lists develop, they can potentially serve as hubs to powerful learning pathways. Additionally, commercial publishing houses are licensing Web access to their curriculum materials for a fee. These online "textbooks" provide material with a stamp of authority, and, as such, strongly appeal to school boards and those who favor limited student choice and control. They also represent an attempt by powerful media corporations to retain control of American learning in the face of the apparent anarchy within the Internet. At the other end of the spectrum, and perhaps more interesting, are the grassroots and freelance efforts on the Web—learning resources created by teachers and students for the school community. These efforts are moving toward a real sense of shared learning, which has powerful implications for the future of the local school.

Even with state and commercial resources and good indexes of materials, classroom and library media teachers will find themselves placing increasing responsibility on students. Classes will become less about what to learn and more about how to learn. Decisions about specific topics for investigation will center less on prescribed subjects within a syllabus and more on subjects that students wish to investigate within a set of choices negotiated by teachers and students. These investigations will tend to be open-ended without a fixed right or wrong answer.

▶ MANAGING RESOURCES

As collection development has become more sophisticated, maintenance issues related to the collection have become increasingly complex. How will resources be processed, organized, stored, retrieved, and used effectively?

While each medium requires some unique challenges (e.g., labeling photographs, magnetically securing software, registering and backing up programs, packaging artifacts), the basic steps of preparing, marking, classifying, cataloging, and storing resources remain the same. The underlying principle is to make resources easily accessible and in good shape for as long as possible. The latter point is particularly relevant for fragile non-print items.

Format is an underlying issue. In the past, libraries often identified and stored materials by format. Remember the filmstrip and microfiche cabinets? Even today, most public libraries have separate video and recording sections—the concept being that people want to view or hear something by format. If only a couple of media are available, this approach may work. However, as more media is incorporated into the collection, the idea of several mini-sections can seem confusing and disparate. As filmstrip/cassette packages became more prevalent, librarians often integrated them into the regular collection or, at least, reserved one shelf per range to keep materials on the same general subject together. While videotapes and audiocassettes lend themselves to that kind of shelving, some LMTs may question the viability of mixing software or CD-ROMs. This is usually a concern about security: do materials need to be kept in a secure place, such as behind the circulation desk or in an office, to prevent theft or other kinds of unauthorized borrowing? Of course, as a result, those materials risk being underutilized. Considering that many non-print resources cost less than some books, the argument for restricting access valuable materials becomes less solid.

When media are represented by only a few titles, libraries also have created separate holdings pages, usually consisting of the minimal cataloging requirements of title, publisher, and date. A good example of existing practice along that line is the ubiquitous periodicals list. Part of the rationalization for such lists is that they mirror the collection's arrangement: by medium. The lists also can help ameliorate the constraints of separate "secure" storage; for example, students can look at the list of reserve CD-ROMs and ask the LMT for a title to use in the library media center. Again, with the inclusion of more media—both in title and format type—the number and variety of title pages can actually impede rather than facilitate access. In most cases, all materials should be fully classified and included in the public catalog to ensure access.

These newer formats push the issue of arrangement to new areas: should materials be stored by medium, by location of accompanying equipment, or by subject? The answer is not as simple as might be imagined. The first consideration is objective—what will be the use of resources? If the answer is research, then the question must be asked: "Will materials be reference only?" Some libraries mix reference and circulating materials. In those cases, non-print items might also be integrated, or they might be placed close to the equipment needed to use them, such as a VCR for videotapes. In library media centers where the reference section or room is separate, again media might be integrated or placed together by the related equipment. Part of the issue is the user's habit of location. Do students think in terms of medium or subject? "I want a videotape on Spain" differs from "I want travel information about Spain." The latter request could be found in books, CD-ROMs, laser discs, videos, or online. The first approach might encourage the LMT to provide a video section, but the second approach might be considered the desirable habit because it focuses on type of information rather than form of information. However, as students develop reports and presentations that enfold a variety of media, their demand for a specific format coupled with a specific informational question demonstrates a sophisticated approach to knowledge building. The LMT must decide what works best in a situation, taking into consideration the following criteria:

▶ school and library mission
▶ educational goals
▶ instructional strategies
▶ ideal and existing use of the library media center
▶ facilities and space parameters
▶ technology access
▶ security
▶ circulation and other policies
▶ other opportunities and limitations.

Policies constitute another management issue. What materials circulate? With the declining cost of technology, replacement isn't as much an issue as pirating and other illegal copying. What are the chances that students will duplicate a tape? What happens if someone accidentally erases a disk? For these reasons, most LMTs choose to limit circulation of such items to staff members, who can be more easily held accountable.

Even the issue of acceptable use within the school or library media center may call for a policy. The Internet is the main scapegoat in this scenario with its wide variance in quality of information. For example, administrators may fear lawsuits stemming from student access to troublesome web sites, so they might prefer less access and more filtering rather than risk legal problems. Librarians, on the other hand, realize the limitations of filters and worry about impeding information retrieval. While the library can be held accountable for the materials it acquires, can it be held responsible for all of the resources that can be accessed from its facilities? Since the question is still out to court, many schools choose to establish an acceptable use policy, which lays the responsibility for access on students and their parents or guardians. Certainly, this approach is more reasonable than filters, which may arbitrarily censor or limit access to sources.

Another important policy deals with donations. Just as book contributions must meet the same criteria for inclusion as purchased titles, technology also should meet school standards. Outdated or broken equipment does not help student learning. Just as the newest edition of a reference work is preferable to an older one, software and hardware need to be updated regularly. And while the fastest system on the market may not be essential, a regular schedule of upgrading ensures the budget accumulation needed to keep the library media center from rapidly becoming technologically obsolete.

Since the advent of audio-visual resources, the library media specialist has dealt with equipment with which to use the needed resources. Over the years, with the ubiquitous nature of AV incorporation, the variety and quantity of equipment have increased dramatically. Perhaps of greater impact, though, has been the increasing speed of equipment upgrades. In the past, a machine lasted about as long as the technology so that the next level of film projector typically corresponded to its mechanical life. In contrast, today's computer can be expected to be outmoded within three years, and most schools do not have the budget to maintain that kind of currency. (In 1994, a 4X CD-ROM drive was tops. In 1997, a 24X drive was typical.) As a result, the LMT has to carefully check the compatibility requirements for software. For instance, a program may need Win98, and if that operating system is not available, the LMT has to decide whether to purchase and install it or to bypass acquiring the software and risk inducing an outdated resource collection.

The attitude about the access and use of these non-print resources also has changed. What was once a classroom or previewing room activity is considered standard practice in today's library media centers. More students learn individually or in small groups hunched around a multimedia workstation in the middle of the library media center. Several facilities issues come to mind:

▶ **Space:** Is there enough space for viewing and production? How will equipment and accompanying furniture be arranged? Have radiation issues been resolved? How is traffic flow managed?

▶ **Furniture:** Is it ergonomically correct? Is it sturdy? Is there enough work space? Does it hide and manage needed cables and other peripherals?

▶ **Electricity:** Does enough power exist? Are there enough outlets conveniently located? Where is the power controlled? How have power outages and static electricity issues been resolved?

▶ **Lighting:** Is it adequate? Can it be increased or decreased depending on need? Is it diffused? Is the location appropriate?

▶ **Heat and ventilation:** Does air-conditioning exist? What degree of ventilation is provided?

▶ **Security and supervision:** Are all resources secure? Does a security system exist? Are work areas easy to supervise?

Particularly with older buildings, the incorporation and expansion of technology can test the limits of a facility, and the changes of any one center or lab can impact the rest of the school's ability to provide the needed power and access to resources and accompanying equipment.

Of course, all of this technology requires human support as well. While today's LMT needs to feel comfortable troubleshooting basic technology problems, having another site person to take care of system or hardcore troubles can be a real lifesaver. Thus, the technology specialist of the '90s has replaced the AV specialist of the '60s. As a proactive measure, the LMT should involve the tech specialist when purchasing resources (both software and hardware) to ensure that the appropriate tech support will be available.

▶ ENGAGED LEARNING

If students are not actively using resources, those resources are basically useless. Reading has set the standard for engagement because it requires a student's attention in order to provide meaning. In a certain sense, video is less demanding because it does not require full mental engagement for students to gain information. However, for students to take complete advantage of the medium, with its sound and movement, they must fully engage not only their eyes and brains but also their ears.

Technology also broadens the concept of access and introduces the possibility of changing resource materials. Books are "done deals." Students can create their own books, and they can quote from existing books, but they cannot (or should not) alter the original book itself. Books also usually are a sequential, linear medium. Presented out of order, they often do not make sense. However, much educational technology is based on random access, which allows students to explore according to individual interests and abilities. Moreover, students may modify some products, such as a hypermedia stack. In fact, some stacks welcome additions and consider the changes as improved products.

Technology goes one step beyond book use in that it allows students to produce their own work while using the technology itself. A whole set of technology is "content neutral," that is, it allows students to enter their own information and shape the product. Typical technology-aided products follow:

▶ Desktop publishing to create a simulated magazine of the day Socrates died.

▶ Spreadsheet program to compare budgets of different families.

▶ Database program to produce comparative information about musicians.

▶ Crossword generator to explore physiology terms or foreign language.

▶ Calendar generators to celebrate diversity.

▶ Graphing programs to analyze criminal factors.

▶ Flowchart programs to trace decision making.

▶ Story generators to describe history in fictional form.

▶ CAD programs to design solutions to urban housing.

▶ Hypermedia program to discuss weather.

▶ Authoring tool to present steps in building a house.

Rather like poetry schemes or literary genres, technology learning tools provide a framework or template with which to organize and synthesize findings as well as generate new ideas.

▶ HIGH-LOAD LEARNING CURVES

To carry that analogy further, the learner has to become aware of and, indeed, comfortable with a structure before using it to shape ideas. Thus, the first time a student encounters a haiku, the issue of 17 syllables can seem more important than the thought behind the count. Developing a skit involves following certain constraints and conventions. It should then be no surprise that technology as a form holds a youngster's attention sometimes before the content matter sinks in or that the first time a student develops a hypermedia stack, more time is spent on colorful backgrounds and fonts than on writing and organizing text.

While there is not a clear correlation between the educational power of a technology tool and its complexity, it is clear that many computer applications and equipment are difficult to master. Consider the difference between creating an audiotape and a videotape. Both are sequential, but the added visual component means that the camera person has to deal with color, exposure, and composition as well as the audio component. Think how easily first graders learn to generate a text on a simple word processor or even an electronic notepad. Now remember the time it took to master PageMaker in order to take advantage of its kerning, wrap-around and import features. And was it worth all the time involved to create that simple newsletter using bells and whistles?

Because teachers want students to con-

Continued on page 30

Connect, Compute, Complete Recommendations

➤ INFRASTRUCTURE, HARDWARE, AND LEARNING RESOURCES

Recommendation 1

Equip every California classroom and school library with the technology resources needed to create a learning environment that will improve student achievement. In an arena changing as rapidly as technology, a too-rigid definition of equipment or material standards risks "fighting the last war." We chose to focus on functionality rather than on specific device features or attributes that would quickly become obsolete. The recommendations that follow represent benchmarks for technological resources rather than a final destination. Although other states also undoubtedly will increase their efforts to integrate technology into their classrooms, we believe that attaining these benchmarks will bring us to the top 10 percent of states. From here, we hope classrooms will adjust their technology upward in support of specific curricula and classroom needs.

The acquisition of the recommended telecommunications infrastructure, hardware, and learning resources will make possible viewing video presentations in individual, classroom, and small group settings; running animation-based simulations; accessing the Internet with evolving digital capability; and preparing multimedia presentations with full-motion and still-frame animation linked to the curriculum. It will also facilitate communication between and among school constituencies—parents, teachers, students, and administrators.

Specifically, we recommend the following:

▶ Telecommunications Infrastructure
Equip every classroom and school library with the telecommunications capability to support interactive, high-speed transmission of full-motion video, voice, and data.

▶ Hardware
In every classroom provide:
- six to eight networked multimedia computers with high-quality monitors
- special interfaces for persons with disabilities
- scanner
- networked laser printer
- 27-inch or larger television monitor
- overhead projector and screen
- telephone

For every five classrooms, provide:
- color printer
- audio recorder
- liquid crystal presentation panel
- video recorder
- videodisc player
- For every 15 classrooms, provide:
- fax machine
- high-speed copier

▶ Learning Resources
Although we do not recommend particular

technology-based learning resources in this report, we do recommend the revamping of the current instructional materials adoption process. The process by which the California State Board of Education currently adopts instructional materials is insufficient to the task of evaluating and acquiring technology-based learning resources. Formulated for an earlier era that was dominated by printed texts, the adoption process is unable to accommodate either the short-term publication cycle or highly focused nature of courseware, CD-ROM, or video resources.

- Adopt a shorter submission cycle.
- Include supplementary materials, not only full courses of study.
- Improve reviewers' technology expertise.
- Establish a network of Web sites for statewide exchange of information regarding learning resources and their effective use in classrooms.
- Set standards for site licensing of software.
- Implement an online "consumer report" for educational materials, accessible by students and parents.

➤ STUDENT CONTENT AND PERFORMANCE STANDARDS

Recommendation 2
Incorporate technology into student content and performance standards recommended by the state for adoption at the district level. In October 1995, Assembly Bill 265 created a Commission for the Establishment of Academic Content and Performance Standards, charged with developing standards that could be required before awarding a high school diploma.

Specifically, we recommend the following:

▶ Extend the mission of this oversight body to include technology-based proficiencies embedded in each content area, at each grade level, and in the design of acceptable mechanisms for testing levels of technology performance including:
- facility with computers and software, such as word processing programs
- the ability to use technology to organize and prioritize complex problem-solving tasks
- the ability to access and gather information from electronic data sources

▶ Use indicators in addition to test scores to measure the overall improvement expected to result from widespread technology integration. For example, businesses can be surveyed to determine their satisfaction with students' job preparedness. Other indicators that must be made part of an annual census are dropout rates, parent participation, attendance, advanced-course enrollment, and participation in scholastic extra-curricular activities.

▶ Require the California Department of Education, as part of a continuous school improvement program, to collect and publish an annual report of technology-related performance statistics not only to benchmark results but also to target additional resources where needed. Such information should be made available at local, state, and national levels.

TEACHER CONTENT AND PERFORMANCE STANDARDS

Recommendation 3

Integrate technology into the content and performance standards that will be used as the basis for setting policies for preparing, hiring, evaluating, and promoting teachers. The ability of teachers to use technology to promote students' acquisition of basic skills and subject matter content is critical to education's success. Accomplishing this objective requires front-end preparation as well as ongoing training opportunities and incentives.

Infrastructure

Specifically, we recommend the following:

- Establish a three-tier scale for evaluating technology competency and use it to monitor attainment of site-specific goals:
  - Level One— Personal Proficiency: ability to use technology for personal use
  - Level Two— Instructional Proficiency: ability to incorporate technology into teaching and learning
  - Level Three— Leadership Proficiency: ability to train colleagues to Level One and Two proficiencies
- Make grants available for staff development within district guidelines.
- Negotiate additional stipends or salary schedule increments for teachers who acquire Level Two and Level Three skills.
- Encourage teacher education programs to train prospective teachers in the use of technology and its integration in their subject areas.
- Encourage students and teachers to act as mentors to enhance technology skills.
- Explore the possibility of requiring Level Two proficiency for new teachers and requiring current teachers to attain Level One proficiency within two years and Level Two proficiency within five years.

TECHNICAL SUPPORT

Recommendation 4

Provide the expertise and resources to support the effective use of technology for students, teachers, parents, and the broader community. Anyone who has ever used a computer knows that sometimes things go wrong. When problems occur, most users have no access to assistance unless they have an expert friend or the number of an industry help line.

Schools with newer hardware may find adequate technical support with one technician per 300 computers. Schools using older installations or those with more challenging needs may require support closer to general industry guidelines, which call for one technician for every 50 workstations.

Specifically, we recommend the following:

- Provide a referral service that includes dial-up help lines, technology specialists, mentors, published materials, and on-site visits to assist in solving technical problems.
- Extend technical assistance to parents and the greater school community by

> - establishing and staffing community technical assistance centers.
> - ▶ Make facilities and technical support available to parents and the community during evening hours and on weekends.
> - ▶ Establish on-line services for frequently asked questions regarding widespread applications.
> - ▶ Encourage development of newsgroups and chat rooms for discussing specific curriculum and problem issues.

centrate on content and ideas rather than on technical mechanics, just-in-time training or the use of reduced load learning curves becomes a viable way to integrate technology and make the learning richer by its use. Again, an analogy to traditional teaching fits well. In early grades, grammar and spelling rules were simple. In early language development, the main ideas are absorbed first, and then finer distinctions are made when the child is ready to assimilate them.

Technology also can be approached that way. Children learn how to push off-on buttons, press keys, and shoot an image. Later they can learn about fonts, composition elements, and editing. If demonstrated clearly, hypermedia stacks can be created within one hour of training. A student can start creating a Power Point presentation after five or ten minutes of instruction. Of course, to use these tools professionally can take hours or months of training. In the process of creating a product, the student may say, "I need to present "x" concept. Will this technology enable me to do that?" That's when the technology specialist or other educator can coach the student, showing him how to make the technology accomplish the task. Because the technique is introduced when needed and used immediately, it gains more meaning and is assimilated more easily. Immediate successful application also helps the student gain self-confidence and willingness to try. The learning curve is manageable. And, more important, the student can concentrate on the ideas rather than splash around in a morass of techno-babble.

Another approach to technical literacy focuses on technology as a medium and takes advantage of natural curiosity. If a student feels comfortable with a word processing program, he may begin exploring its advanced features, such as HTML capabilities or drawing options. Later documents can then make use of these added elements to show more sophisticated ideas. This open-ended exploration actually reinforces the concepts of experimentation and cause-effect relationships. Students can transfer this spirit of learning to their course content. "I wonder what would have happened if the South had won the Civil War?" or "I'd like to learn more about plants."

Each idea is contextual with relation to other ideas, to culture, to personal experience, and to the form of the idea's presentation or delivery. Technology makes this point absolutely irrefutable and obvious. What's more, it enables students to expand their own learning tools (e.g., sight, kinesthetics), connect more fully with ideas, and control their learning.

States are attempting to meet student needs by recommending technology that can be integrated into existing curricula. The recommendations of the California State Library Task Force exemplify the broad-based interest in technology's role in education.

Netscape Guidesheet

1. **Connect!** Make sure you have a way to connect to an Internet provider, either by modem or high-speed line.

2. **Start Netscape:** Locate and double-click on the Netscape icon. It opens to the home page. Scroll down the screen to read the information.

3. **Link to a site:** Links are "hot text" that connects you to another page. You access the page you want by clicking on the different-colored or underlined text.

4. **Use an address:** If you know the address to a location or site you want, you can type it in. (It's sometimes called a URL: Uniform Resource Locator.)

5. **With Netscape, click the "Open" button.** A dialogue box will pop up for you to type in the complete address.

6. **Search:** Click on the "Net Search" button to activate a search engine. Each search engine is a program that looks for documents that have the topic you're looking for. Common search engines include WebCrawler, Lycos, Magellan, and InfoSeek. Some search engines allow Boolean strategies. Use "Net Search" for unambiguous or multifaceted topics, such as "mononucleosis" or "Chinese filmmakers." If your topic contains two or more words, enclose them in quotation marks or parentheses so the search will link them together.

7. **Click on the "Net Directory" button to activate a series of topical menus.** By clicking on a topic link, you can narrow a broad topic to a highly focused one. Use "Net Directory" when you want to narrow the kind of databases to be searched, such as "Mars" when you want just the planet and not the candy bar.

8. **Bookmark.** Want to go back to a particularly useful site later? Find Bookmark, and click on it. Drag the mouse down to "Add Bookmark." This stays on the system; you can even export the Bookmark onto a floppy disk to take elsewhere. (On other Internet browsers, "Bookmark" may be called "Favorites.")

9. Quit Go to File, and drag the mouse down to "Quit." Sometimes the term used is "Exit."

NOTE: While this explanation tells how to use Netscape, Internet browsers are generally similar. Terminology may differ, but the process is basically the same.

> **HOW DO YOU TRANSLATE A URL?**
>
> **http://Calacademy.org./~library/gbalc.html** translated is: *http://* is the protocol (e.g., hypertext transfer protocol). *Calacademy* is the host computer. *org* is the type of system (e.g., organization). *~library* is the directory where the information is stored, and *gbalc.html* is the Web page or file. *html* means hypertext mark-up language.

From *Training Student Library Staff*, p. 144.

Generic Protocols for Electronic Resources

▶ MENUS:

- ▶ Menus act as tables of contents.
- ▶ They are located on the opening screen or along one edge of the screen.
- ▶ Main menus often divide into more specific sub-menus.
- ▶ Menus can refer to different topics, approaches, or computer functions.
- ▶ A menu bar at the top of the screen is often called a navigation or pull-down bar.
- ▶ To use, click on the term and drag the mouse down to the desired highlighted option.
- ▶ Sometimes, the option can be activated by pressing a function key and letter simultaneously (e.g., ctrl-C).

FUNCTION KEYS:

- ▶ Function keys are non-alphanumeric keys that allow the user to perform certain tasks.
- ▶ Sample keys: enter, control, delete, tab, alternate, page up, page down, arrows, option, command, and print
- ▶ Some keyboards include "F" keys, usually F1 to F10 or F12. These are located at the left or top of the keyboard. They are often program-specific, and enable the user to perform tasks such as print or save.
- ▶ Sometimes the user has to press two keys simultaneously to activate the action, such as "ctrl-alt-del" to reboot a DOS computer system.
- ▶ HELP is a special function. It might be activated by F1 or by "command-H." Help can range from tips for specific screens to an electronic tour of an entire program. Sometimes Help is available at the specific point of need; sometimes it is one general screen of hints.

▶ PRINTING:

- ▶ Most electronic resources let the user print the information.
- ▶ The printer command is located in the menu bar, usually under "File" or at the bottom of the screen as a function key (e.g., F6).
- ▶ Usually, a portion of an entry can be printed by highlighting it and using either a "Print selection" option or going to the print dialog box and choosing a "Print selection" option.
- ▶ If an option is grayed (e.g., not in black type and not possible to highlight), then it can't be done. This happens sometimes when the user wants to print a picture.

▶ IF SOMETHING DOESN'T PRINT, LOOK FOR THESE COMMON SITUATIONS:

- ▶ The printer is off.
- ▶ The printer is not connected to the computer.
- ▶ The printer is out of paper.
- ▶ The wrong printer has been chosen.
- ▶ If several computers are linked to one printer, it may take a while for the printer to get to the job at hand.

▶ The printer driver has not been installed (least likely and most technical reason).

SEARCHING:

▶ "Browse" searches alphabetically like an index. This approach works when the user doesn't know the exact wording or spelling (e.g., "Michelangelo").

▶ Basic "Search" allows the user to type in a word for the computer to match with words in the program and retrieve the information. This approach works when the user has a simple topic to search or wants to see how a topic is related to other similar ones (e.g., "television").

▶ Boolean Search allows the user to type several words or phrases together, linking them with AND, OR, or NOT. This approach works when the user wants to narrow or broaden a topic or to find a specific relationship between two concepts (e.g., "spider" and "web").

From *Training Student Library Staff*, pp. 102-103.

Generic Principles in Using Slide Projectors

▶ SET-UP:

▶ Set the projector on a stable surface.

▶ Loop the power cord once around a leg of the projector table, cart, or stand before plugging it into the outlet. (This prevents the cord from being yanked out accidentally.)

▶ Attach the remote control device.

▶ If the projection lens is stored separately, carefully insert it into the projector.

▶ Place the slide tray in the correct starting position on the projector. For carousel projectors, the tray slot on the bottom should be aligned with the selection slot on the machine. Check the placement by testing a slide or two.

▶ Set the projector at the desired distance from the screen or projecting surface. (The greater the distance, the larger the projection.)

▶ Turn the projector focus knob the to get a clear image.

▶ Adjust the elevation knob to get the best placement. The image should be above most viewers' heads, yet not so high that the image becomes distorted (keystoned).

▶ Check the lighting level, so the image does not look washed out.

▶ Turn the lamp switch to the fan level when not projecting slides. Some machines have an low light option that can prolong bulb life.

▶ SHUT-DOWN AND MAINTENANCE:

▶ Turn the lamp switch off, but keep the fan going a little while after finishing the slide show. This allows the bulb to cool.

▶ Remove the slide tray before turning off all the power unless you are certain that the tray and machine slots are aligned perfectly.

▶ Screw the elevation knob all the way back flush with the machine.

▶ Screw the lens all the way back flush with the machine, or remove it carefully if it is to be stored separately.

▶ Disconnect and wrap all cords carefully, and store them properly. Some projectors have a built-in storage space.

▶ Store the projector in a case, and transport it carefully.

From *Training Student Library Staff*, p. 109.

Who Shall Lead?

Just as it takes a village to raise a child, so it takes the entire school to educate a child. The one-room schoolhouse with one teacher managing the education of all the village's children has given way to a team of educators and other support personnel guiding students along a personalized educational path. Leadership has become a team effort. As worksheets and multiple-answer tests have been replaced by substantive projects, all educational stakeholders must plan together to ensure seamless instruction and accountability.

➤ WHAT IS THE WORLD OF THE STUDENT?

All people are born learners. From the beginning, they respond to their surroundings and adjust in order to have their needs satisfied. At first, the repertoire of responses is limited—cries and gurgles. However, additional techniques quickly come into play as children learn to speak, behave, and otherwise cope with and then shape their environment.

In their most narcissistic state, children see others as their figurative servants. The world is available, waiting to be explored freely. Adults are useful for facilitating that exploration: by providing tools, translating words, explaining the unknown, acting as a social buffer, and keeping children safe. Parents are the gatekeepers who size up the goodness and relevance of other adults. Teachers are the next group of helpmates. To the consternation of some personnel, younger eyes often do not distinguish between teacher and aide, professional librarian and clerk, network certification and AA degree, secretary and principal. To the student, either adults are helpful and kind, or they are not. It is up to these adults to define their own roles and work together to help children grow to be resourceful and contributing members of society.

➤ PARTNERS FOR LEARNING

In the most general perspective, every person within the school helps to make learning possible. Maintenance personnel keep classrooms safe and clean, providing a sense of order. The nurse helps students stay healthy, and intervenes when a child needs medical attention. Cafeteria workers offer healthful meals. Secretaries facilitate communication and other daily operations. Administrators oversee the smooth running of the school. Parents support their children's efforts. However, the key educational players are the classroom teacher, the library media specialist, the school technology specialist, and the student.

Together they determine the student's needs, both academic and social. Together they structure the learning environment. Together they determine what resources are available.

▶ THE TEACHER'S ROLE

Probably the main influence in students' lives is the teacher. Because of their daily interaction, students and teachers form a close relationship. As such, teachers know students' competencies, and students work to gain teacher approval. Besides being content specialists, teachers also sense group dynamics. Because teachers are bound to instructional outcomes and frameworks, they generally set the parameters for research projects and other learning experiences.

▶ THE LIBRARY MEDIA TEACHER'S ROLE

Two facets define the library media teacher's niche—resources and access to those resources. Because the LMT works with all students, across all disciplines, she supplies a longitudinal study of general student progress. The LMT is also in the best position to see and facilitate cross-curricular learning experiences. Particularly in high school settings, teachers may become so departmentalized that they may neglect to find out about other coursework. World cultures and foreign language may well both be developing travel brochures for the same geographic area. History and English classes may be studying the literature of the same time period. Science and physical education may both be exploring sports science. Think how much more enriching a project can be when the student can relate it to several contexts; the work can deepen and, in effect, teachers can "cover more ground" knowing that the student is exposed to concepts in another course.

▶ THE TECHNOLOGY SPECIALIST'S ROLE

Of rising importance in the teaching partnership is the technology specialist (TS). Remember the AV guy of the '50s and '60s? That job largely disappeared in the '70s with major cuts in school library budgets, but it has been transformed into a technology position. In some cases, the technology specialist focuses on hardware installation, maintenance and troubleshooting. In other cases, the TS instructs students and teachers in technology use. Similarly, a TS's background may range from a high school degree to a teaching credential, from a willing parent volunteer to a full-time engineer type, from self-taught to Novell Certificate graduate. Depending on the school's culture and needs, the TS's role becomes an extended experiment in matching people and tasks.

Usually the TS "corners the market" in the technical and operational aspects of technology-based resources and facilities. As such, the TS supports the learning effort by maintaining the technology environment. If the TS helps instruct users, the content of instruction is typically desktop publishing, file management, and other basic computer literacy skills. This expertise frees the teacher to concentrate on the content matter of the technology and how to incorporate it into the students' learning experience. It also allows the LMT to focus on teaching how to research, evaluate, and select information.

On the other hand, a more high-powered position, such as Technology Coordinator, might well entail a strong curriculum and training expertise. This kind of expert tends

TASK	CT	LMT	TS	CLASS
Develop Content Outcomes	X	X	x	x
Develop Social Outcomes	X	X		x
Develop Indicators	X	x	x	x
Develop Assessment	X	x-X	x-X	x
Develop Pre-requisite Skills	X	x-X	x-X	
Diagnose Pre-requisite Skills	X	x-X	x	x-X
Determine Available Resources	x-X	X	x-X	x
Determine Teaching Methodology	X	x-X	x-X	
Determine Time and Place	X	x-X	x-X	
Finalize Learning Experience	X	x	x	x
Assess Learning Experience	X	x-X	x-X	x-X

(CT = Classroom Teacher; LMT = Library Media Teacher; TS = Technology Specialist; CLASS = Class of students; X = Major player; x = minor player)

to coordinate both hardware and software selection and acquisition, train teachers in the use of tools as well as their integration within the curriculum, and head up technology planning. The role then becomes more administrative in nature, and it begins to resemble the LMT's administrative role.

▚ THE FABRIC OF AN EDUCATIONAL PROGRAM

A table serves to graphically represent the interdependent roles of each educational player in the planning and implementation of an overarching educational program.

Each task involves several issues:

▶ **Develop Content Objectives.** What should students learn to know and do? Regardless of the instructional method, students grapple with specific subject matter. Each discipline has its own vocabulary and slant on knowledge. In counterpoint, specific information literacy skills cross traditional curricular lines, providing means to access, evaluate, and manipulate content material. As teaching teams develop learning experiences, they should meld those two perspectives, so students can improve both process and product. Educational technology comprises aspects of both content and information literacy as witnessed by the number of computer-related courses that emphasize the computer as an end in itself. A more forward-looking attitude is that technology facilitates access, use and presentation of content. Educational technology should be chosen carefully and aligned with the content and information literacy objectives; for example, accessing or creating an audiocassette about evolution probably would be as educational sound—

or as interesting—as accessing CD-ROM information and producing a hypermedia presentation on the topic.

▶ **Develop Social Objectives.** If cooperative learning is part of the picture, then social or maintenance group outcomes also must be determined. In typical outcomes, all group members participate in creating a HyperStudio stack; the group stays on task; groups learn how to prioritize facts; all members are responsible for ensuring that the entire group understands a key concept. The LMT should be consulted to make sure that facilities and hardware lend themselves to group work.

▶ **Develop Indicators.** What does the learning look like? How can you tell that a student has mastered a skill? What level of competence is acceptable? Rubrics offer specific descriptions that characterize the desired process and product. Different rubrics may be needed for each aspect of learning outcome—content, information literacy and technology skill.

▶ **Develop Assessment.** What will be assessed? Who will assess? How will assessment be conducted? When will assessment occur? Team development implies team assessment, and each of the above questions needs to be discussed and resolved. Naturally, the assessment should align with the outcomes, but it also needs to provide feedback along the way so the learning experience can be modified to maximize positive results.

▶ **Identify Pre-Requisite Skills.** What skills do students need to accomplish the task at hand? For instance, to present a Power Point debate requires that students know how to manipulate that software program. If they don't, then either that skill needs to be taught—to a few or all of the class—or another presentation tool needs to be used. Likewise, students can't list current trends in a social issue if they don't know how to find magazine articles or use the Internet—two information literacy skills. Nor can students determine the causes of the Cold War if they don't know what that "war" is. Too often, educators assume prior knowledge by their students only to witness too late students floundering and missing assignment deadlines because they need to catch up on learning an associated skill or concept. It is far better to establish time at the start to learn associated skills or to rework the assignment, so that smaller steps incorporating other skills can lead to the culminating project.

▶ **Diagnose Pre-Requisite Skills.** The more the entire learning team, including students, can diagnose pre-requisite skills, the more successful the ultimate learning experience will be. Particularly when the LMT and TS interact with the same students over time across the curriculum, they can help the classroom teacher and students determine the right content and level of instruction. The ideal situation is one in which each student is challenged reasonably. Of course, not every student is at the same stage simultaneously. However, a substantial project can take advantage of student heterogeneity and peer coaching. For instance, a videotape of a skit in French can make use of varied student skills in small cooperative groups—speaking, vocabulary, creative scripting, acting and directing, videotaping and editing.

▶ **Determine Available Resources.** What materials do students need in order to learn? Resources include information in print, non-print, and human form.

Resources also include technology software, hardware, and facilities. Resources imply items for presentation—paper, communication tools, and tapes. Do resources take into account the variety of student learning styles and processes? Where are these resources located—in the classroom, the library media center, a lab, or off-site? How accessible are they? Do they require guidance to use them? Are other people, such as another class, in competition for the same resources? Can more resources be acquired or borrowed? Do existing resources need to be modified for the particular learning experience?

▶ **Determine Teaching Methodology.** How will the lesson begin, and how will it engage students? Based on the pre-requisite skills, topics for instruction may need formal introduction or brief review. A range of teaching aids must also be considered: from transparencies to group panelists, from demonstrations to packets of self-paced guide sheets, and from audiocassettes to interactive computer tutorials. Are these teaching tools available, or do they need to be prepared or acquired? Who will provide these aids or other instruction? Ideally, team instruction blends content and skill. Any team member may be called upon to lead the group processing or to coach individual students, depending on the need.

▶ **Determine Time and Place.** Particularly with team instruction and school-wide learning projects, a variety of spaces may be envisioned—alongside negotiated scheduling of time. How much time is needed for instruction and practice and for group work and presentation? What is the time commitment of each team partner? Where will the activity take place? Students may begin planning in the classroom, locate information in the library media center or lab, gather opinions in the community, organize findings in the writing lab, and present in an auditorium. Each site may call for different material and human resources and may be needed by other classes or for other projects. Each team member needs to remain flexible about the learning experience and its ultimate "shape."

▶ **Finalize Learning Experience.** Taking all factors into consideration, the classroom teacher is the most likely coordinator of the assignment. Particularly when it includes imbedded content matter, information literacy and technology skills, as well as social or group tasks, the assignment can effectively meld these elements and associated outcomes into benchmark projects.

As the table demonstrates, the relative importance of each person's role needs to be negotiated for each task or subtask. Ideally, the desired outcomes and instructional needs, based on the level of student expertise, should constitute the critical factors driving the mix of players; however, several other issues influence the combination, such as:

▶ site, district and state frameworks, and standards,

▶ the availability of the Internet (including whether the Net has crashed),

▶ scheduling of facilities—library and technology labs,

▶ time constraints—other school activities,

▶ expertise of each educator,

▶ willingness to cooperate by each educator, and

▶ cross-discipline impact.

Particularly with learning experiences that cross subject areas, the richness of potential student learning is matched by the challenge of coordinating such projects. In any case, one classroom teacher needs to have ultimate responsibility for scheduling and coordinating the learning experience.

ASSESSMENT

As outlined above, assessment issues occur at the beginning of the lesson design. What is being learned is intimately connected with how that learning is assessed. Each educator brings to the process her own perspective and skill, which should be included in assessing the entire process and product. Ideally, each educator should assess the part for which she is responsible—the LMT assesses student research strategies and uses of resources; the TS assesses use of technology; the student assesses cooperation within the class group; and the classroom teacher assesses the progress in content knowledge. Each player needs to determine how to assess his particular contribution as well as the knowledge gained by the student. Some of the methods include:

▶ demonstration of competence (e.g., ability to create a HyperStudio stack),

▶ observation of student effort (e.g., research strategies),

▶ objective test (e.g., comprehension of content), and

▶ peer assessment (e.g., contribution to group effort).

Assessment shows not only how well students achieve but also how well the process works. Ongoing assessment enables instruction to be re-directed or fine-tuned to improve student work. Team teaching is especially beneficial because peer observation can provide valuable insights into the process and can facilitate quick, improved modifications.

Any assessment should be clear, descriptive, accurate, specific, and focused on the achievable. Educators also need to assess how well they contribute and work with their project team mates. Some indicators include:

▶ Frequency and length of interaction: Does the team meet regularly to plan?

▶ Depth of contribution: Is input substantial?

▶ Variety of interaction: Does everyone engage in the full inquiry cycle?

▶ Effectiveness of planning: What decision are made, and how are they implemented?

▶ Use of human resources: Is the full range of expertise acknowledged and used?

▶ Degree of responsibility: How does the team share responsibilities?

▶ Impact of partnership: How does participation influence student achievement and team development?

▶ Conflict resolution: Are tough issues confronted and solved?

Ultimately, the entire school is accountable for its students' education. The educational team models the learning community. Different educational experiences demand changing teams, but the total effort should reflect a long-term commitment to each student and staff member to learn in the most effective way possible—together.

Literacy in the Digital World

In the digital world, what do we mean when we talk about the literate person, the well-educated citizen? Some technology critics have been heard to say, "With computers, students won't have to know how to read or write. They won't learn how to spell. They'll have a push-button education." Some teachers probably wish it were that easy. Instead, young people need to be even more literate and more discriminating than ever before. If students misspell a word, they won't find what they're looking for on the Internet. If they can't read, they won't be able to evaluate a Web site. If they can't write, they won't be able to share their findings.

In fact, technology reinforces and drives the concepts of literacy, expanding them to new educational horizons. Reading literacy, perhaps the historical core of literacy, has broadened to include information literacy in this Information Age. The early twentieth century concept of visual literacy has been co-opted by the larger idea of media literacy. Other literacies are sprouting on the scene: computer literacy, scientific literacy, emerging literacy, adult literacy, and cultural literacy.

The educational heart of these literacies remains the same—the ability to comprehend, analyze, interpret, and interact with ideas. The important point is to distinguish between ideas by responding to content, form, and context. Technology introduces more forms in which to express ideas. Thus, students need to be aware of these subtle differences and build a greater repertoire of literacy skills. Fortunately, technology also can facilitate this skills building.

▶ WHAT'S IMPORTANT?

We want our children to be the best informed youngsters on the planet. Yet, alarmists today produce facts and figures to demonstrate that students fall far short of this goal, and newspapers are filled with articles telling us of California children who cannot find the Pacific Ocean on a map and other similar horrors. This "knowledge gap" has produced two different solutions—a back-to-basics approach, reducing curriculum to "essential literacies" (Hirsch), and a performance assessment approach, seeking to grade students on demonstrations of knowledge (Sizer).

Both schools of thought call themselves "essentialist," which causes some confusion and leads to the question of defining what is really essential in the digital world. The first school of thought confines knowledge to lists of information (e.g., when did Columbus sail?), practices (e.g., diagramming complex sentences) and algorithms (e.g., long division) that students must master. These lists, practices, and algorithms, packaged for teachers and students, are set forth in the traditional school mode defined by classes, bells, and the like. They return school to the linear analog world of the past and do not require high levels of technology for success. They are orderly, cheap, and easy to access—and they are appealing because they speak to what we have traditionally thought of as knowledge. Unfortunately, they are out of date in the world of high school neutral information strings.

In a world where information doubles every year, how can experts repackage the essential list? How do you decide which dates are critical? What is more essential—Adlai Stevenson or John Van Neumann? Diagramming sentences or keyboarding? Knowing how to divide or knowing when to divide? When the tools of learning change every 18 months, how do you decide which practices to teach? Where calculators have replaced pen and pencil calculations, what is the need for using old algorithms? The best the experts can do is to package the essentials of 50 years ago. Such packaging will not move American students to the top of the world class.

▶ NEW INDICATORS OF LITERACY

How do we know if someone is literate? Here are some of the indicators of information literacy as noted by the American Association of School Librarians:

The student can:
- ▶ access information efficiently and effectively:
  - ■ identify informational needs accurately
  - ■ locate potential sources to satisfy informational needs
- ▶ evaluate information critically and competently:
  - ■ assess the authenticity and usefulness of selected sources
  - ■ comprehend and extract needed information from the sources
  - ■ analyze the implications and draw conclusions from the sources
  - ■ evaluate the process and product thoroughly and realistically
- ▶ use information effectively and creatively:
  - ■ synthesize and organize informational findings to satisfy informational needs
  - ■ integrate new information into one's existing knowledge base
  - ■ apply information to decision-making
  - ■ share their information accurately and convincingly to an audience.

In its most basic form, literacy has to do with mindfulness—the meeting of minds and the making up of one's own mind. One connects to the ideas of another person by either reading, viewing, or otherwise experiencing the communication. Then one deals with the ideas—ignoring them, refuting them, understanding or misunderstanding them, and integrating them. Finally, one decides whether or not to apply the synthesis/results of that original meeting/connection to meet with another mind in a sort of thoughtful cycle or spiral.

While no direct mention is made of the medium or the context, certainly they are embedded in students' ability to access, process, and apply information physically and intellectually. We know that information does not exist in an intellectual or emotional vacuum. Both sender and receiver of ideas exist in a context of time, space, environment, culture, and situation. The idea itself is wrapped in some delivery mode, so not only do minds have to contend with the ideas themselves, but the form of delivery as well.

The digital world has exploded those delivery forms. Each one shapes ideas and transforms them differently. It is difficult enough for students to sort literary genres and types of writing, e.g., scientific or philosophical. With the advent of video, hypermedia, and digitized sound, students have to sort the qualities of each new medium that translate an idea uniquely.

▶ MEDIA LITERACY

People have always had to respond to a visual world. In fact, aural and visual conventions have been part of societal lessons for centuries as part of human instincts. Pre-literate humans understood the oral tradition of storytellers and the emotional connotations of body parts. The classical world included the symbolic language of icons and statues. In more recent history—say, the Renaissance—"artificial" rules for visual representation, such as one- and two-point perspective, were introduced.

However, the formal educational focus on visual instruction didn't start until the twentieth century with the introduction of visual mass media formats of moving pictures and sophisticated photography. One key was the integral role that mechanics/technology played in visual production and display/presentation. In addition, these mass media technologies were placed, for the first time, in the hands of the masses themselves. Schools consciously started to examine the educational elements of these media. As advances in communications models, systems analysis and learning theory, including behaviorism, influenced visual literacy, so too did technology make gigantic strides—more in society than in education. Media literacy today often refers to the critical analysis of television. The impetus seems to be on advertisements' covert or societal messages complementing the TV programs although the shows themselves certainly reflect particular social values, which may or may not align with formal educational intentions. The spirit connotes consumerism rather than media production or another type of call to action.

One recent definition of media literacy was generated at the Annenberg School of Communication in 1992: "the ability to choose, to understand, to question, to evaluate, to create and/or produce and to respond thoughtfully to the media we consume. It is mindful viewing, reflective judgment" (Megee, 24). Specific elements that a media-literate person responds to include:

- visual elements: composition, color, shape, line, text, movement
- audio elements: tone, rhythm, speed, loudness, clarity
- attention elements
- symbols and connotations
- organization: sequencing, timing, grouping, emphasis
- complexity: of content, format.

But if students are to be producers of media as well, then they need to know how to manipulate the elements listed above to create an original product. Indeed, the possibilities for sharing findings have increased dramatically. The five-page report has been replaced by a grocery list of product possibilities:

- written: poem, story, essay, article
- visual: poster, bulletin board, storyboard, comic book, slide show, photograph album
- multimedia: brochure, hypermedia stack, slide-tape program, videotape
- musical: song, chant, composition

- symbolic: graph, chart
- kinesthetic: skit, dance, game, play
- manipulative: puzzle, diorama, booth.

LITERACY ISSUES

We've already looked at a couple of issues that involve literacy: media and context. Another major shift in literacy is its focus on student construction of meaning. Folk tales, for example, were stories that subtly taught societal norms. Early mass education was needed to prepare young people for employment—to know the work ethic and basic skills to perform a job. More years were needed to educate youth because society was becoming increasingly complex; more knowledge was needed in order to survive successfully. In each case, young people were treated as passive, or at least open, recipients of information and values; they were being taught how to fit in.

One aspect of newer information literacy deals with the critical assessment of information. Previously the print world was considered more or less sacrosanct; the idea was that the "Establishment" knew best. When librarians selected material that was fit to be read by students, information literacy focused more on intellectual access. Now a major task in literacy is to question the information itself—not just how useful it is but how valid it is. In other words, young people cannot rely on society to judge what is right. There is no one intellectual dogma or canon. Rather, criteria for judgment or assessment have replaced "the right answer."

The constructivist educational theory turns on that mind set. Education is arranged to provide a learning environment in which young people explore a rich set of ideas and possibilities. They then construct meaning from the offered material and create a personally significant product. The teacher facilitates this exploration by setting up a structured, stimulating environment and helping students gain skill in using literacy tools to explore their surroundings. As a result, information literacy emphasizes process rather than "the right answer," and student-centered issues rather than institutionally-driven norms or abstractions.

A significant part of the process emphasis raises another literacy-related issue—cooperative or collaborative work.

- **Identify the information need.** By eliciting ideas from several people, more existing knowledge as well as more questions for learning can be generated.
- **Develop a research strategy.** Different students can pursue a topic from different points of view, access points can multiply, and students can redirect their peers upon need.
- **Access information.** Students with different learning styles and intelligence can relate more easily to different types of information.
- **Evaluate and interpret information.** Students can draw upon the experiences of their peers to better assess sources; the possible rise of conflicting interpretations can lead to deeper understanding and more profound resolution.
- **Synthesize and organize information.** Students may specialize by task, such as writing, drawing, and layout.
- **Present information.** A bigger or more complex product can be produced and shared because more talent is available to share the task and clarify findings.

Increasingly, students need to know how to work well with others. Peers become sources in themselves and can provide valuable information and insight. Young people need to learn how to access, evaluate, and make good use of those human resources. The fact that most people learn from each other and that they work on complex tasks that necessitate coordinating specializations gives credence to this aspect of literacy processing. Each step in a research project, for instance, can be enriched through small group work.

Cooperative learning also brings up the issue of diversity—believing that all students can learn and encouraging the varying attributes of students. From "hard-wired" or innate differences to personality idiosyncrasies, each student brings a unique perspective to the learning "table." Students can build their literacy skills from their

ATTRIBUTE	TEACHING STRATEGY
Physical:	
left-brain dominance	Use time lines, provide general theory, give practical applications
right-brain dominance	Draw pictures, engage senses, do skits
auditory learner	Use verbal directions, assign oral reports
visual learner	Use overhead projector, employ handouts
kinesthetic learner	Use manipulatives, emphasize note taking
field-dependent	Provide context for learning, use cooperative groups
field-independent	Use classification schema, encourage inductive reasoning
Mind styles:	
concrete-sequential	Give step-by-step directions; provide hands-on learning
concrete random	Experiment, use CD-ROMs in learning environment
abstract sequential	Encourage codes and ciphering activities, teach deductively
abstract random	Explore feelings, give "the whole picture"
Multiple intelligences:	
linguistic	Lecture, give written projects
spatial	Explain with videos and demonstrations, produce charts
musical	Encourage poetry, encourage "rap" reports
kinesthetic	Use games, encourage use of equipment in projects
logical	Design experiments, develop puzzles
social	Use simulations, encourage peer coaching
intrapersonal	Incorporate reflective journaling, encourage self-paced projects
naturalist	Encourage observation, use classification systems

strengths, and then feel comfortable in improving their less-developed areas as they fine-tune their literacy tools. Here are just a few ways that students differ—and ways to help those students learn:

The most important implication for educators is to provide a variety of sources and help students connect and respond to these resources in a variety of ways. Technology potentially increases the odds that students will succeed.

THE ROLE OF TECHNOLOGY IN LITERACY

With the advent of equipment-dependent informational sources, use of technology has become a subset of information literacy. The user needs to know how to access the source and then navigate through it using the equipment and strategies such as Boolean searching and formal communication protocols.

With those skills, though, students can significantly broaden their repertoire of information literacy tools:

- by utilizing more senses separately and simultaneously—kinesthetic, aural, visual,
- by accessing more sources from around the world,
- by communicating more effectively and in more ways, and
- by attempting more substantial projects involving more sources and more people.

As with cooperative learning, the incorporation of technology colors and enriches information literacy throughout the research process:

- Identify the information need by using email, online discussion, and idea-generating software.
- Develop a research strategy by assessing data gathering resources and using project management software.
- Access information through search engines, navigation tools and by conducting online surveys.
- Evaluate and interpret information by comparing sources, understanding URL conventions, and asking other experts.
- Synthesize and organize information through desktop publishing, authoring and presentation programs, database and spreadsheet programs, Web pages, and CAD.
- Present information through application programs (see above), telecommunications, video and audiotape, and images, such as photography.

COMPUTER LITERACY VS. INFORMATION LITERACY

As beneficial as it is to introduce computers into education, this change also raises the issue of computer literacy, which, for some educators, takes precedence over computer use. This attitude leads schools to offer computer literacy classes that train students in overall management of the machine, and introduce them to some basic computer programs or, in some cases, to computer languages. While these classes produce students who can operate computers, they fail to assist students in core classes. The argument for these classes is that students need to learn the machine before they can use it. This philosophy is derived from the implementation of other complicated technologies in our society, such as learning to drive a car before using it in a pizza delivery job. But even then, most drivers really don't know the inner workings of a car—just as a student doesn't need to know about computer registers.

Ten years ago, there might have been some validity to this argument about machine management, but most systems that schools use are quite simple, and little instruction is required for students to be able to work with them. The Internet is a point-and-click system with a graphical interface that is usually intuitively accessible. Most work processing programs have basic entry levels of use, and anyone with rudimentary keyboarding skills can type a file, save it, and print it. Granted, all programs require practice for mastery, but studies show that development of skills moves more quickly when there is immediate need for the skills. Computer labs that are used for learning programs, not using them for meaningful work, tie up labs that could be used school-wide and produce "computer literate" students who never use computers for their schoolwork.

Technology use in the classroom is predicated less on student understanding of how to operate computers and more on teacher understanding of the computer as a medium for learning and expression of that learning. Computer programmers spend a great deal of time developing interfaces that are intuitive and easy to understand. The more professional the software, the easier it is to learn. Professionals have little time to waste learning a new program; they need to be immediately productive. It is possible to break down most software into basic components, and allow students to develop their understanding of the program as they work on projects that have personal meaning. This approach eliminates the need for spending large amounts of time on a learning curve devoted just to the software and more time on thinking and learning about the subject of the course.

In a recent classroom project in which high school juniors were asked to use the Internet for researching documents from early American history, the teacher began by asking how many students had computers at home. Most students raised their hands. Next, the teacher asked how many students regularly "surfed the Net." Some hands went down, but most hands stayed up, indicating that the class had a fairly sophisticated understanding of the Internet. Finally, the teacher asked how many students every used the Internet for schoolwork. All hands came down. Not a single student had used Internet resources for school projects. The problem for these students was not one of access or of understanding how to use the tools. The problem was that no one had ever asked them the kind of questions for which the Internet could provide answers.

Students need experiences or assignments that allow them to discover that the Internet is an appropriate choice and to understand when other resources better suit their needs. For example, P. E. students wanted to search the Net to find out who won various matches at Wimbledon in a given year. The librarian let students first explore online; she then showed them how to find the information more quickly using an almanac.

The moral of this story? Students have less chance of becoming information literate if schools do not define those skills and provide students with opportunities to learn to use literacy skills. Moreover, students will not make effective use of their skills—and the technological tools to hone those skills—if meaningful projects do not demand the incorporation of those competencies.

CHAPTER 7

Presenting...

Shared leadership lays the groundwork for a school-wide learning community, a real life environment for intellectual growth. The emphasis is on openness and collaboration rather than on closed door policies, on experiment rather than lecture, on open-ended discovery rather than prescriptive facts, on connections to the world rather than ivory tower abstracts, and on a continuum of learning rather than discrete chunks of educational blocks. In short, this learning community scenario turns traditional education on its head.

Another angle in this educational picture is the anchor point—student performance—which is the ultimate test. While education has always tried to prepare students for the future, the method of measuring that preparedness has varied. Especially in large institutions, standardized objective tests have often been used to measure learning. Interestingly, traditional apprenticeships most closely approximate the "new" concepts of authentic performance—significant and complex student work that shows real-life application.

WHAT DO WE MEAN BY "INSTRUCTION?"

The word "instruct" comes from the Latin word for building, the connotation of structure. The teacher, thus, builds the structure or knowledge base for student learning. The age-old problem for the teacher has been how to draw the essentials from the core of knowledge of a given discipline and disseminate it efficiently to a group of youngsters whose experience with that knowledge is limited. In pre-literate times, the method was entirely oral. Knowledge was in the possession of the master, and techniques, such as the Socratic method and mnemonic devices for stimulating recall, were developed to further students' understanding and retention.

Historically, where pedagogy differs is in the type of structure. In some circles, the teacher builds the entire conceptual building, and the students get to know the idea structure by intellectually stepping inside. In other circles the teacher builds the conceptual *framework*, which the students then fill in with the supervision of the teacher "foreman." The "sage on the stage" describes the intellectual building, and the student is expected to reproduce the artifice. In some cases, that is still the more efficient way to get an idea across—say, a quick introduction to an author. But even in classical Greece, Socrates taught conversationally, drawing out student insights and building ideas with them.

The development of the book introduced the first crack in this top-down structure. First, students no longer had to memorize all of the information since a reference source was now available. In addition, books gave students some independence from the instructor since "live" lectures and dialogues were no longer the only source of information. Just as traditional instructors did not give the computer a warm reception, instructors in ancient times railed against books. Plato himself thought that books "destroyed memory." This resistance, however, did not prevent the book from becoming an educational tool as teachers found themselves supplementing their lectures with text, selecting appropriate readings for each discipline, and working with librarians to provide students with sources of greater depth. With the invention of the printing press, the ratio of books to students improved dramatically. Yet, while the technology of the book shifted the role of teacher from sole source of information to facilitator of information, the goal of the process remained the same—to provide students with knowledge of the core elements of a discipline.

The twentieth century witnessed the expansion of the public library, the addition of school libraries, and the availability of textbooks for each student, which combined with a changing social fabric to encourage students to expand their knowledge by working on their studies outside of class. Gradually, this capacity expanded so much that homework became an essential part of pre-college education. This system was reinforced by the fact that in most disciplines the core body of knowledge had expanded to such a degree that students could not achieve mastery within school hours. Once again, the teacher's role shifted. A clerical function was added, and a certain part of the instructional day was used for assigning and collecting homework, as well as checking homework for correctness and understanding. In the process, the teacher moved closer to a facilitator role, and students gained a further measure of independence.

However, the educational system remained largely unchanged. There was an agreed understanding of what knowledge students needed to acquire, and the teacher—a master of the discipline—determined how students acquired it. While students were given some latitude on when they could learn, there was never any thought as to latitude on what they should learn. In a class of 30 geography students, on any given day all of them would be studying the same geographic elements of the same corner of the world.

Enter the desktop computer. Of course, it has not revolutionized education overnight. It is a developing technology that is expensive and sometimes difficult to implement. Its continuing development means that we still don't know its ultimate power, and we have not yet been able to firmly define its role in the educational system. But it has already altered the way we think about what instruction should be, and its introduction helped foster the image of "teacher as facilitator."

What have been some of these changes? The networked computer grants a great deal of independence to students, providing almost unlimited access to the core knowledge of disciplines. It alters the manner in which information is delivered, breaking away from pure print environments and offering an enriched environment that includes graphics and sound. Through access to world-class databases, students are freed from local restraints. Furthermore, networked computers have made possible the rapid addition of new information to the core knowledge structures. These additions have been democratized to such a degree that one can find the thoughts of a Nobel Prize winner indexed alongside the notions of a third grader.

Through high-speed electronic indexing systems, the networked computer allows high-speed manipulation of data, which, in turn, provides greater sophistication of analysis and synthesis. On the other hand, the touch of a button reprints entire texts, which, depending upon its accuracy, may contain all of the information that a teacher has asked a student to discover on a given question. Frequently, there seems to be little reason for students to puzzle answers for themselves.

This new access has confused many educators as to their role as instructors. In the forest of information, where are the trees? What constitutes mastery these days? In most disciplines, the body of knowledge is expanding faster than students—or teachers—can absorb. Even basic premises and first principles are under attack in some disciplines while uncertainty prevails in others. This is as true in the humanities as it is in the sciences as shifts in the canon of authors have redefined essential readings, and global perspectives have replaced Eurocentric approaches to social sciences. If teachers are to justify their role in the classroom, they must take a proactive approach in helping students deal with the ever-growing body of knowledge—and misinformation—that confront them.

In short, instruction now requires an equal emphasis on *how* to learn and *what* to learn. Teachers must break away from the standard combination of lecture and assigned readings followed by a test. In order to provide students with a repertoire of learning strategies, the concept of instruction must be broadened to include demonstrations, simulations, role-plays, and numerous other strategies. The choice of instruction method is determined by the lesson's objective, the group's setting and time frame, the students' prior knowledge, the resources available, and the probable succeeding unit. As the philosophy of "guide on the side" has gained strength, more emphasis has been placed on structuring a learning environment in which students can designate resources and construct meaning from them. The teacher helps students process their experiences and draw viable conclusions from them at the point of need. The *how* of education has become as important as the *what* of education. Timeliness, the "golden teaching moment," has gained pedagogical respect as well. In fact, recognizing when a student needs help and knowing how to intervene meaningfully to redirect a student's efforts is a core skill when incorporating technology into the curriculum.

▶ THE STUDENT'S VIEW

From the student perspective, instruction requires a shift in thinking as well. How do high school students survive in an environment that increasingly calls for independent learning? Involved in a job, sports activities, and an intense social life in addition to school, how can they be expected to make sense of the vast domains of information and organize it sensibly? Isn't it far better to provide students with pre-digested blocks of knowledge, no matter how limited, simply to help them keep things straight? The answer is yes since textbook summaries of essential basic learning are still useful, and probably required, in most courses. But in the Information Age, textbooks constitute the beginning of knowledge, not the end. The information in a textbook chapter in American history can only provide a baseline of knowledge for students. After reading that, students must step out on their own to learn more, test this new knowledge, form opinions about the information, and evaluate them against those formed by their peers. It is not so much the textbook chapter that needs to be rewritten as it is the questions at the chapter's end. These need to inform students that there is a wider world beyond the chapter and provide pathways into that knowledge. Until such books are written, it is up to teachers to help their students onto the paths.

INSTRUCTION FOR STUDENT LITERACY

Library skills instruction exemplifies changing instructional practice. In the past, it was sometimes considered a separate subject, but most educators would now agree that library skills have been replaced by information literacy skills, and that instruction should be embedded in meaningful contextual learning. No more: "Reader's Guide on Tuesday," but rather "How do we find current articles on social issues of concern to today's teenagers?" The same skill is being taught, but the rationale and approach have changed considerably.

A discovery approach to information literacy also points out a possible danger in this kind of pedagogy: that such just-in-time training may lead to the student never receiving the instruction. In a way, the concept of constructivist learning has to be compromised a bit when educators agree that certain concepts and skills are needed for all students by the time they graduate. The trick is to make sure that "just in time" is scheduled somewhere into the curriculum. The actual instruction itself may occur in several ways and by several educators. The process is straightforward:

1. Gather all educational stakeholders, e.g., a representative from each department or grade, library media teacher, and technology specialist.

2. Examine and analyze present student work, from assignment to final product, in terms of literacy issues.

3. Come to consensus about information and media literacy skills that students should have and at what point.

4. Identify where introduction, instruction, and practice now occur and where gaps now exist.

5. Determine where the needed learning will occur.

6. Develop a scope and sequence for literacy and communicate it throughout the school. Implement the plan.

7. Evaluate the plan and its implementation.

This model of curriculum development and outcomes management can be applied to the broadest bases of education while still recognizing the individual needs of students.

HOW CAN WE TELL STUDENTS ARE LEARNING?

In order for learning to occur, students have to change—either inwardly or outwardly. They gain knowledge; they change attitude; they become more skilled. The key lies in how students demonstrate their learning and what systems of measurement we put into place to document that learning. If knowledge is based on recall of facts and computation of problems, then multiple-choice tests may suffice. In fact, if all the necessary facts are on a CD-ROM or DVD disc, and a computer program can solve all the math problems, then it may be more important to know how to run software. But even the best memories are flawed, and everyone makes mathematical mistakes. And with the massive amounts of information now required for a sophisticated understanding of the world, it seems even more essential to have students demonstrate their knowledge through critical manipulation of information rather than reciting the information itself. Multiple-choice tests must, therefore, be ruled out.

Instead, demonstrations of learning, as with instructional methods, have increased in variety and depth; moreover, they are frequently the result of a group effort. The most obvious method is by *doing* something. In order to have real-life application, these demonstrations or *performances* should approximate the actual situation as closely as possible for maximum transference of learning. This kind of performance is called *authentic* performance, and aligned assessment of that behavior is called *authentic assessment*.

While such practical indicators of learning seem logical and reflect an apprentice model of learning, schools have long used paper-and-pencil tests and ScanTron multiple-choice exams to assess student learning. Why? Lack of time, increased number of students, heavy teaching load, and belief in standardized and norm-referenced tests. This last factor may be the least educationally sound because the chief concern should be how well students master a skill or concept, not how they measures up to other people.

With the incorporation of technology, students have a greater repertoire of performance tools. Some of their options include:

▶ videotaping an interview or job shadowing experience,
▶ photographing a nature study,
▶ presenting a slide-tape show about another culture in the community,
▶ creating a hypermedia presentation on a political campaign,
▶ audiotaping an oral history,
▶ creating a magazine or newspaper about an event or date in time,
▶ designing a CAD blueprint of a house, or
▶ developing a CD-ROM about dating decision making.

In each case, the product involves a complex set of skills, knowledge, and attitudes. Students have to know how to synthesize and transform information. They have to determine an appropriate format for presentation and how to fit their findings into that medium. The project is often sophisticated or large enough that it requires team effort, which in itself involves social and academic collaborative skills. Such demonstrations often are used as culminating experiences of mastery learning, but they also need to occur throughout the year, so teachers and students can assess their progress and change instructional and learning directions accordingly.

Middle School Technology Sequence
A Scope and Sequence of Skills to Be Implemented Within Curricular Studies

OPERATION AND CARE

MIDDLE SCHOOL GRADES: 5 6 7 8

Equipment/Hardware
Skill	5	6	7	8
start up and shut down hardware	●			
manipulate mouse to point, click and drag	●			
apply basic troubleshooting techniques	●	●	●	●

Operating System

File Operations
Skill	5	6	7	8
edit a file and save changes	●			
delete a file	●			
rename a file without the use of "save as"	●			
copy a file from hard disk to floppy and vice versa	●			
copy a file form disk to disk	●			
format disk	●			
use keyboard shortcuts in place of menus	●	●	●	●

Transition between computer platforms
	5	6	7	8
	○	●	●	●

ETHICAL USE
Skill	5	6	7	8
demonstrates appropriate behavior while using equipment	●	●	●	●
respects the privacy of other students' data & work space	●	●	●	●
respects copyright laws			●	
treats disks & equipment with respect			●	

APPLICATIONS

Authoring Tools

Keyboarding
Skill	5	6	7	8
recognizes letter keys	●			
function keys:				
option/alt, command, function, num lock	●			
fingering conventions:				
home keys				●
keyboard - locates keys with correct fingering				●
touch typing				●

Word Processing
Skill	5	6	7	8
use spell checker	●			
use thesaurus	●			
cut, copy & paste	●			
insert header/footer		●		
place graphics & text together in documents		●		
import graphics		●		
import text		●		

	5	6	7	8
set margins/tabs		●	●	●
adjust vertical spacing and alignment		●	●	●
adjust page orientation		○	●	●
insert footnotes			○	●
use style sheets		○	●	●
use desktop publishing to produce documents: e.g. newsletter, flyer, booklet		●	●	●
Databases				
explain two uses for databases		●	●	●
communicate using database vocabulary		●	●	●
organize data (sort)		●	●	●
retrieve data systematically		●	●	●
collect, record, and add data (information)		●	●	●
interpret data		●	●	●
analyze data by finding patterns		●	●	●
discovering relationships		●	●	●
making inferences		●	●	●
create and test data file		●	●	●
create a report within the database		●	●	●
print		●	●	●
Spreasheets				
explains two uses or more for spreadsheets		●	●	●
communicates using spreadsheet vocabulary		●	●	●
enter data		●	●	●
use of mathematical operators		●	●	●
plan	○	●	●	●
create	○	●	●	●
edit	○	●	●	●
produce graphs	○	●	●	●
print	○	●	●	●
Mutlimedia tools & presentations				
record sound	●	●	●	●
storyboard/plan project		●	●	●
create new *HyperStudio/HyperCard* stack, construct text		●	●	●
create fields, buttons, graphics		●	●	●
import graphics		●	●	●
import sounds/record from audio sources		●	●	●
import digitized video movies		●	●	●
computer control of laser disc player		●	●	●
animation (see cross-ref in graphics)		●	●	●
create links to connect to other programs		●	●	●
connect to telecommunication programs		●	●	●

MIDDLE SCHOOL GRADES

	5	6	7	8
Graphics				
Painting programs				
merge graphic with desktop publishing	●	●	●	
merge graphic with word processor	●	●	●	
import/export files	●	●	●	
edit saved graphic	●	●	●	
Drawing/drafting programs (e.g. MacDraw)				
communicates using related vocabulary	○	●	●	●
rectangle tool, line tool, fill pattern, duplicate	○	●	●	●
demonstrates function of draw/paint tools	○	●	●	●
merge drawing with desktop publishing	○	●	●	●
merge drawing with word processor	○	●	●	●
import/export files	○	●	●	●
edit saved drawing	○	●	●	●
print	○	●	●	●
Rendering programs (e.g. Photoshop)		○	●	●
Animation - 3D animation		●	●	●
Graphing calculators			●	○
Audio				
record 8-bit sound with microphone (see Multimedia)	●			
use cassette recorder to record and play back sounds	●			
record and edit 16-bit sounds	●	●	●	●
use synthesizer with MIDI imput to computer		○	●	●
record and mix sounds from peripheral sources		○	●	●
Motion Video				
record a video using a video camera	●	●	●	●
edit video using in-camera editing techniques	●	●	●	●
use laser disc player to view laser discs	●	●	●	●
use remote control		●	●	●
edit videotape using two VCRs		○	●	●
play and record QuickTime/.avi technology				●
Other Digital Media				
use flatbed scanner & software		●	●	●
use scanner & optical character reader (OCR) software				○
use digital camera and software		●	●	●
use PhotoCD ™ with CD player		●	●	●
use CD ROM discs with CD drive on computer		●	●	●
Design and Construction Tools				
plan scope and sequence of a project using storyboard or design brief		●	●	●
construct a project using Computer Aided Design (CAD) software		●	●	●

	5	6	7	8
use mechanical tools to solve a problem	■	■	■	■
use simple machines to conduct an investigation or solve a problem	■	■	■	■

Robotics

	5	6	7	8
use computer to control light/sound		○	■	■
programming robotic devices: e.g. Lego Logo or FischerTeknic		○	■	■

RESEARCH AND CONCEPT DEVELOPMENT

Curriculum Specific Software

	5	6	7	8
use appropriate curriculum-based software	■	■	■	■
use computer simulations within the curriculum: e.g. Oregon Trail	■	■	■	■

Research Tools/Information Retrieval

	5	6	7	8
use division of information into categories as a research tool	■	■	■	■
use table of contents, index	■	■	■	■
conduct a subject search in library using CD-ROM, on-line databases	■	■	■	■
access databases on-line with telecommunications (see cross-ref)	■	■	■	■

Telecommunications & Networking

	5	6	7	8
use of network for printer sharing	■	●		
use file sharing over network	■	■	■	■
use of network for access to telecommunications	■	■	■	■
modem use	●			
demonstrate proper etiquette	■	■	■	■
conduct research on-line	■	■	■	■
use boolean logic to conduct a search	■	■	■	■
use key words to conduct a search	■	■	■	■
use search engines	■	■	■	■
use directories	■	■	■	■
use electronic library resources	■	■	■	■
send and receive E-Mail	■	●		
"chat" on-line	■	■	■	■
use bulletin board services; access, read, send & receive files	■	■	■	■
access the World Wide Web	■	■	■	■
download files	■	■	■	■
view and save "source" materials	■	■	■	●
construct home page for use on the World Wide Web	■	■	■	●

We recognize that not every school has the equipment to implement these recommendations. Please use the planning sheets included to adapt them to your particular site and student needs.

OUTCOMES, BENCHMARKS, AND STANDARDS

What should students be able to do and know—under what conditions? This is the baseline question for every school learning community. As workshops and multiple-choice tests give way to projects incorporating complex sets of skills, it falls increasingly to the teacher and support team to determine the quality of work and the depth of understanding.

Similar to behavioral objectives, student outcomes identify *who* does *what* at what point in *time* to what *degree* of proficiency. Unlike behavioral objectives, which specify a percentage of students within a class, outcomes apply to *each* student. Additionally, outcomes usually refer to broad-based competencies rather than specific, discrete activities. For instance, the Tamalpais Union High School District established 14 exit outcomes—essential skills and concepts that graduating senior should demonstrate. Within each course, dozens of behavioral objectives might be developed, each of which is aligned with the major outcomes. In fact, student outcomes should drive curriculum development and educational practice. It makes sense: to spend school time on the things you want students to learn.

Because outcomes are so general, they need to be fleshed out with *descriptors*, which identify the main intended performance, and *indicators*, which specify the desired behavior. A descriptor solidifies the outcome—solve mathematical problems, use economics in daily life, or express oneself creatively. An indicator specifies the required performance or product—a multimedia presentation, a monologue, a science fair project, or a debate. As much as possible, the performance should approximate a real-life situation; the more that school-based learning resembles real world tasks, the easier it is for students to transfer and apply learning outside of school. If outcomes express exit competencies and indicators specify the final product, then it is a good idea to include *benchmarks* to mark progress toward the final goal. Grade-level portfolios constitute typical benchmarks because they show examples of student work throughout the year and provide a means for students to self-assess their yearlong progress. Likewise, a culminating year-end project can serve as a benchmark although a benchmark project at mid-year may be better timing since it allows students and teachers to redirect learning efforts for the rest of the year.

Standards is another word that is bandied about in educational and political circles. The standard specifies the desired level of competence—solving ten problems correctly in five minutes, justifying a conclusion with five pieces of evidence from three different perspectives, or reading 15 books in a year from six different genres. There is great debate about the basis for standards—national, statewide, district wide, or grade-specific. The underlying concept is that standards provide a means to measure and compare performance across classes and personalities. In practice, standards usually are general statements. Content standards most closely resemble outcomes. Performance standards correlate to outcome indicators. Sub-component standards refer to benchmark measurements.

If standards establish the "bar" of excellence by which students are measured, then *rubrics* provide a concrete means to measure how far from the bar their performance now stands. Currently, the most common correlative to rubrics is the A-through-F grading system. In this system, the teacher describes the performance for each letter grade, from an "A" (e.g., an error-free oral report with excellent presentation style, based on accurate and thorough coverage of the topic) to an "F" (e.g., no report, or random talk with no preparation and no content). At present, the school community often doesn't understand how grades are determined. Teachers need to work together to establish published school-wide standards and rubrics and to educate parents and students in their use. Ideally, students receive the performance rubric at the beginning of the unit, or they help devise it. They then use the rubric to measure their learning during their activity. In that way, a rubric can be used as a formative assessment that gives a snapshot view of progress and helps the student modify or advance individual effort. Of course, the rubric itself should not be the goal; rather, it indicates behaviors relative to a desired outcome at that point in time. (See sample on pg. 64)

To add to the complexity, while states and local entities are currently working feverishly to establish outcomes and benchmarks, the technology keeps moving the target. It is the task of standards committees to provide exemplars in an environment that is continually changing. It is no wonder that the report of the California Model Technology Schools is entitled *Building on Shifting Sands*. Inevitably, this situation causes problems in a system where codification of standards has been considered essential to the proper running of schools. How do we determine an "A" on an animation created by sixth graders when a couple of years ago sixth graders couldn't do animation? How can we deem a third grader who creates a Web page a failure—no matter how thin the content? If a sophomore can solve all of the problems in the pre-calculus course using a computer, do we make that student take the course next year if the only difference is that the same problems will be solved without the computer program? At best, these standards will not appear overnight, and in the meantime we have to put up with some uncertainty. But schools that are deeply involved in the process will fare much better than schools that ignore the discussion or rely on the state to do their job.

In a recent conversation with the authors, David Fowler, professor of educational technology at the University of Nebraska, suggested a simplified set of standards that could ease the frustration of the benchmark debate. Pointing out that the authors of HyperCard recognized five levels for the use of that multimedia program, Professor Fowler suggested that current benchmarks could easily be grouped around these five levels and that they were appropriate activities for students at every grade level.

Early adopters of multimedia in the classroom will recall that HyperCard established the following five user levels—browsing, typing, painting, authoring, and scripting. While these five levels no longer represent all the varieties of multimedia to be found, they do represent categories of activity levels for students to master. Browsing represents the ability to retrieve information by traversing a sequence of screens. As this skill develops, students learn to search for specific information and to cross reference sources. Typing represents the ability to manipulate text, whether through cutting and pasting of source material or the generation of original text with a keyboard. Painting can be expanded to include all of the various graphic media, from jpeg (Joint Photographic Experts Group compressed format for still image transference) to Quicktime video with sound. Authors use multimedia software to build their own presentations while students learn scripting to add levels of complexity to their work through the use of computer languages from Logo to hypertext to Java. These user levels easily translate into a simple set of skills for benchmarking students and can be taught in all grades at levels that are developmentally appropriate.

▶ RAISING THE BAR

Already much talk has been made of *improving* education standards. "Students aren't learning enough." "Standards should be set high, so students can reach up to them rather than set at a minimum that anyone can achieve without effort." Obviously, educators and the community at large want students to achieve and be competent to their fullest extent. The problem arises when standards are set so high that a significant proportion of students might not meet those standards. Are the school and community willing to live with the consequences—lack of diplomas leading to dead-end jobs or higher dropout rates or litigation against institutions for failing children? High standards require an equally high-quality support system to act as a safety net for low-achieving students.

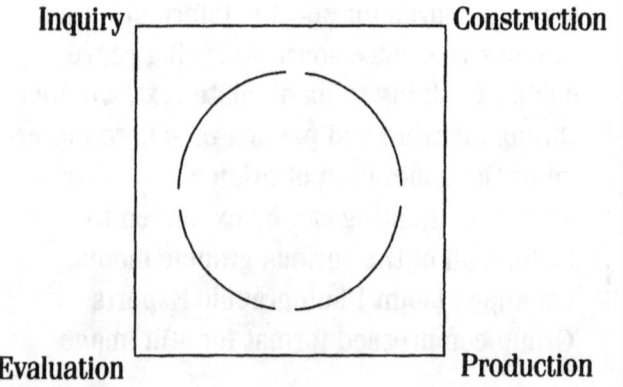

CYCLE OF INQUIRY

Inquiry — Construction

Evaluation — Production

More effective than raising arbitrary standards is student-initiated product improvement. When students know that they have a real audience for their work and when they create projects that are personally meaningful for them, they are more apt to put forth their best efforts to show what they know. And when they see the fruits of prior classes' efforts, current classes challenge themselves to do even better. In this scenario, students start out by examining the standards that provide the first end point and the rubrics that let students know the direction to the end. Their final product becomes the new concrete "bar" of excellence for the next class. Like the Olympics, the anchor project establishes the record for the next group to break.

▶ CYCLES OF INQUIRY

Student "bar-raising" practice corresponds roughly to the professional practice called the cycle of inquiry. Basically, educators gather data—typically by examining student work and their own efforts—and draw educational conclusions. Since high performance is the goal, educators look for patterns of achievement or lack of achievement. They disaggregate the data to isolate the factors or subgroups of success or failure. For instance, freshman boys may constitute 75 percent of all incoming high school students who do not meet writing standards. The next step is to hypothesize the underlying reason for the learning gap. One factor may be that of organizational skill. This hypothesis may be tested by comparing the organizational structure of the writing samples of boys and girls. If the pattern exists, the next step is to design an intervention or action plan for the targeted audience. Following this scenario, teachers might decide to pay extra attention to content organization by showing students

Technology Indicators (K-12)

➤ OUTCOME:

Use technology as a tool to access information, analyze and solve problems, and communicate ideas.

➤ DESCRIPTOR:

The student demonstrates competence in the use of authoring tools, graphic applications, and telecommunications. Uses technology in many disciplines to solve problems. Selects and employs a variety of electronic technology resources for research and communication. Creates products using technologies. Uses technology responsibly, legally, and ethically.

➤ TECHNOLOGY CATEGORIES:

Authoring Tools:
- word processing
- desktop publishing
- databases
- spreadsheets
- multimedia programs

Motion Video:
- camcorders/editing
- laser disc player
- QuickTime/avi or equivalent
- Video Toaster or equivalent

Audio:
- 8-bit recording with microphone
- 16-bit audio recording/editing
- synthesizer
- mixing/recording peripheral sources

Graphics:
- drawing programs
- painting and rendering programs
- CAD
- animation (3-D)
- graphing calculators

Digital Media:
- graphic scanners
- optical character readers
- digital video cameras
- PhotoCD™

Robotics:
- computerized light/sound
- programming robotic devices

Telecommunications:
- conducting research online
- downloading information
- online communication

Design & Construction:
- design briefs
- graphic design tools
- mechanical tools
- simple machines/engines

Future Technologies:

➤ INDICATORS:

Graduation:
- Within a curricular context, the student will produce a solo project that exhibits mastery of the following technologies:

authoring tools, graphics, and telecommunications, plus items from at least two different technology categories. Students may propose projects that encompass such processes as design, construction, and modeling. Or the student will develop a portfolio that incorporates the use of three or more technology categories with sample works from at least four subject areas.

■ The student will meet standards and pass the Tam District Computer Literacy Test in all five sections.

■ The student will present documentation proving responsible, legal, and ethical use of technologies used in project preparation. The student will write an essay using a word processor describing a situation in which technology is or has been used inappropriately. The student will then describe how the situation may be rectified to make it appropriate and legal. The student will discuss the implications of the illegal actions.

Eighth Grade Benchmark:

■ The student will produce a cross-curricular solo project utilizing at least three authoring tools plus three other technologies.

■ The student will present documentation providing responsible, legal, and ethical use of technologies used in project preparation.

Fifth Grade Benchmark:

■ The student will produce a cross-curricular project presented by a small group, utilizing at least two authoring tools plus two other technologies.

■ The student will present documentation providing responsible, legal, and ethical use of technologies used in project preparation.

Second Grade Benchmark:

■ The student, either individually or in a small group, utilizes technology to express understanding of a topic using basic word processing, graphics, and recorded sound.

■ The student demonstrates responsible and appropriate behavior while using technology.

how to use graphic organizers, and giving specific guidance on written assignments. (Note that the action plan is carried out regardless of gender; the assumption is that boys will need to be corrected more than girls.) To see if the intervention worked, the next step would be to retest the population and compare results. While the cycle could be closed at that point, with all students meeting writing standards, or the cycle could spiral instead because the first inquiry might lead to questions about related work, such as reading—or explore other means of expression, such as verbal. The underlying purpose remains to raise the bar on student learning and on educational practice. And on the classroom level, when used as exemplars, student work challenges the work of following classes. Students actually lead the cycle of inquiry ensuring that sound educational practices continue and improve.

▶ REAL LIFE LEARNING

This is real-life learning. Complex projects with meaningful standards and ways to demonstrate mastery educate students in a variety of problem-solving skills that will help them when they reach the real world. This kind of learning addresses the needs asserted in the 1991 U.S. Labor Secretary's Commission on Achieving Necessary Skills (SCANS) report—the ability to productively use resources, interpersonal skills, information, technology, and systems. In the real world, when shipments don't arrive or equipment breaks down, quality suffers. Anyone who has worked in a production facility understands. But it is interesting that some folks in the educational system, which was modeled on factory thinking, don't understand this. In the real world, students who have learned to work with groups have learned to gather and synthesize information, then select the appropriate technology for presentation, whether it is in engineering, business, or medicine. Thus, the reduction of learning to a teacher-lecture-textbook-test system without outside "interference" results in simple functioning, but it does little to educate students in skills beyond those of recall.

One difficulty facing the educational world is the problem arising from documenting student success. As we leave the world of the standardized test and letter grade, and enter a world of performance-based rubrics, it is difficult to rank students—the traditional method for determining who is ready for which college. In an age of multiple college applications, it is not possible for admissions officers to interview every applicant or read extensive essays. Recent assaults on the validity of SAT test scores may render them less effective in determining student preparation. What can be done?

This is actually a much larger issue than one of mere record keeping and standardization. The whole educational system, from kindergarten through graduate school, needs to be overhauled, with pathways created to help all students find avenues for success. As we develop new forms of digital storage, standardizing these new record-keeping forms may be as important as creating new assessments. Electronic portfolios of student work are already being developed, which may well be the ultimate arbiter of student progress. Storage is no longer the problem—a single ZIP disk can store a student's entire set of high school English composition and most of his other school work, including research and lab reports. A student with hefty multimedia or graphics portfolios can choose from several mass-storage devices, similar to JAZ drive cartridges. Read-write DVD probably gives most students a career's worth of storage space.

In short, digital building blocks with which we now create information structures have altered the way we accumulate, manipulate, and evaluate knowledge. Various forms of new media have created new skills for students to master. The need to access the connections to knowledge databases has altered the school structure, school community relationships, and assessment. While individual learning no longer requires a book or a lecture or even a teacher or a school, it still requires management and ways to evaluate. For the organized education of our mass population, schools will still be necessary for managing learning programs and measuring progress. Digital media makes this management possible. Staff development helps make the evaluation valid. A sample educational outcome (from the Educational Task Force of Marin County, California) with specific indicators is on pages 61 and 62.

Technology and Product Rubric

Outstanding: 4	Highly Competent: 3	Competent: 2	Not Yet Proficient: 1
complexity in defining problem and stating thesis	clearly defines problem/states thesis	defines problems/ states thesis	does not define program/state thesis
accesses relevant information from wide variety of sources	accesses relevant information from diverse sources	access relevant information	does not access relevant information
shows thorough understanding of the problem, concepts and processes	shows good understanding of the problem, concepts and processes	shows general understanding of the problem, concepts and processes	shows little or no understanding of the problem, concepts and processes
provides an exceptionally clear, coherent, complete, and organized explanation	provides a clear coherent, complete, and organized explanation	provides a reasonably clear, coherent, complete, and organized explanation	provides an unclear or incomplete explanation
rarely contains technical errors contains relevant information	contains few technical errors contains relevant information	contains some technical errors contains relevant information	contains many technical errors contains very little information
uses correct language mechanics and usage	uses correct language mechanics and usage	uses correct language mechanics and usage	contains many errors errors in language mechanics and usage
production and composition are excellent	production and composition are good	production and composition are fair	production and composition are poor
integrates diverse technology effectively	integrates technology effectively	integrates technology	does not integrate technology

From Marin (California) Educational Task Force

Multimedia Reporting

The traditional system of education calls for the repetition of a cycle familiar to everyone who goes to school. The teacher gives an assignment; the student works on the assignment and returns the assigned work to the teacher, who then verifies its quality and accuracy. The student receives a grade and a new assignment. Periodically, the teacher tests the student on a body of knowledge covered by the curriculum. The average of the graded assignments and test scores constitutes the measure of what the student has learned. This cycle works well in the analog world of print. In the digital world of multimedia, however, it is inadequate at best and has been replaced by the cycle of inquiry discussed in earlier chapters.

Words and numbers no longer comprise the major building blocks of knowledge. Students now manipulate sounds, graphics, video clips, and other icons and symbols beyond the world of text, and they must work differently with these digital representations of knowledge. New skills are required, and classroom procedures need to be altered accordingly. For example, teachers require their students to take notes on lectures in class. But if the "lecture" is an online presentation of a series of three-dimensional shapes and patterns generated by a mathematics program, there are few notes to take. Instead students must concentrate on observing the patterns, and then must learn to manipulate the program in order to explore the mathematics represented. The knowledge comes from understanding the visual complexity that equations can generate, both aesthetically and mathematically.

Given the wide variety of media that students must manipulate in the course of an assignment, there also are a number of methods through which they can report their level of understanding in a given subject. Students need to learn a variety of information skills, so they can share their findings effectively. Organizing these skills and developing processes for information manipulation is the job of the instructional team. Without adequate organization, multimedia projects break down or become so time-consuming they lose their instructional value. Properly prepared students, however, produce work at a high level—work that is marked by novelty, complexity, and sophistication.

▶ ORGANIZING THE PROJECT

It is important to recall that in the cycle of inquiry the assignment is orchestrated

Contract

I, _____, promise to fulfill my contract by completing the requirements of the Global Systems and Interactions Project. By signing this document, I am accepting the responsibility to perform in the individual as well as group tasks as stated below.

1 Our geographic area is:

2 My other team members are:

3 I will be researching (circle one):

    Humans and their Environment   Animals and their Environment

4 The species I have chosen is most commonly known as:

5 I will be following the calendar and checklists to stay on task. I know that I must take notes on all printed material. My notes and bibliography will be graded. Highlighting printouts does NOT constitute taking notes.

6 I will be presenting my individual information by (choose one):

    Essay   Day in the Life of...   Travel Diary   Newspaper   Become It

    Diorama   Video with Script   Pretend Interview   Field Notes (pretended observing)

7 My individual project will include:

    a. Answers to the questions for my species

    b. Bibliography (sources in correct format)

    c. Visuals (pictures/displays)

    d. Reflection (to be done after the entire project is finished)

8 I will collaborate with my group members to put together a group project starting on April 20th (the day the rough draft of my individual project is due) and completed by April 30th.

I have read and understand the terms set forth in this contract. I realize by signing this, I am accepting the responsibilities stated above.

_____   _____
(Student Signature)   (Date)

I have read the Parent Letter and this Contract.

_____   _____
(Parent Signature)   (Date)

through collaboration with the students. Student goals determine the success of the project and need to be clearly defined from the beginning. The practice of requiring student design briefs—templates for describing the parameters of a project—are now becoming a standard method for monitoring student inquiry sessions. Student contracts, a set of agreements describing the levels of student participation, are another method for determining student accountability from the outset. Design is a critical step in project organization. Unfortunately, it is a step often ignored by teachers and students alike. Without it, breakdown is inevitable. Storyboards, which may be simple four-panel depictions of project outcomes, or elaborate flowcharts outlining information processes, assist students in the initial phases of project creation and allow teachers early assessment opportunities.

▶ THE CYCLE OF PRODUCTION

The cycle of production mirrors the cycle of inquiry. Students establish an essential question, determine what they need to know, select and extract information, refer to their storyboard to identify gaps, discuss problems with the learning team, conduct more research and analysis, and begin building their multimedia product. Throughout this cycle, essential multimedia skills, from browsing to scripting, are called into play. The tendency of these processes to overlap has led many observers to refer to this kind of learning as "messy." And yet, as the process becomes more refined, the student is able to develop real precision of analysis and depth of understanding while producing a sophisticated demonstration of knowledge.

While much of this process is self-directed, the learning team of classroom teacher and library media teacher works with the students, making careful note of progress and assisting students over hurdles. Additional expertise also may be available from the school technology specialist or online through software Web sites or by e-mail to experts. The atmosphere is extremely collaborative and requires engagement by all participants. A teacher who leaves the research to the librarian, or a librarian who works with the catalog and not the students, fails to teach and may create insurmountable difficulties for students. In a working partnership, there is an opportunity for real teaching to occur—working with small groups or individuals, answering the questions of the curious, discovering insights with the thoughtful, and providing encouragement and motivation for the reluctant. Much of the teaching consists of modeling learning behaviors. Teachers and librarians demonstrate that they are learners too, by participating in the joy of discovery. As the information is gathered and sorted, as digital building blocks are created by the students, and as the assembly of a new knowledge structure begins, everyone benefits.

▶ USE OF FACILITIES

The creation of multimedia projects can put a strain on school facilities. While many students have computers at home, many do not. Therefore, teachers need to understand that assembling such projects will be done at school, with supplemental work—typing text and reference material, for example—completed at home or during extended library hours. In addition, many teachers lack the requisite number of computers within their classroom for every student to participate in full-dress multimedia production, even as team members. Thus, while teachers can originate such projects in their classrooms, they must rely on the school media center and technology labs for completion. Knowing

MARCH / APRIL

					27 Kick-off and topic selection	28
29	30 First group meeting 6th	31	1 Library twice and homework one night per subject.	2	3 Note check, source list, contract due	4
5	6	7	8 Library twice and homework one night per subject. Bibliography	9 Research done Check notes	10 No school	11
12	13	14	15 SPRING BREAK	16	17	18
19	20 Rough draft due	21 Begin team work using modified schedule after 1st period	22 Materials Ind. Proj. Feedback	23	24 Final draft due	25
26	27 Board check	28	29 Final days of modified schedule Project completed	30	1	2

☐ = Checkpoint

---

how much time to book in each of these facilities for a given project requires experience, and coordination with the library media teacher and school technical support people is essential. Ideally, these personnel join together as a learning team and work together on project design. And there is much work to be done. Web sites need to be bookmarked. Appropriate authoring software needs to be selected and managed. Files should be created on the school server; and print material and artwork may need to be digitized. While some of this work can be delegated to students, other aspects require that adult personnel take charge.
Collaboration in the planning and use of facilities is a critical aspect, and many projects are derailed when the school environment does not foster this collaboration.

▶ MOMENTS OF BREAKDOWN

Despite the number of computer glitch jokes and the occasional highly-publicized computer malfunctions, computers have evolved into fairly reliable machines. But universities, hospitals, the stock exchange, major corporations, air traffic control systems, and nuclear power plants operate daily with the assistance of computers, and desktop machines, when used correctly, do not crash with any high rate of frequency. Still, in planning multimedia projects, teachers need to take safeguards against moments of breakdown, which may occur.

Of all the computers apt to cause difficulty, public school machines rate near the top of the list. These machines are frequently low-budget models with marginal maintenance whose users may not have much training in their use and sometimes have no concern for the machine's well-being beyond the need to complete a given project "now." School networks are also apt to be balky as well as being serviced by overbooked technology specialists. And users of these systems may not understand their operation. Both classroom teachers and library media teachers must recognize the necessity of well organized, properly maintained hardware and networking systems. All members of the school community must foster a climate that shows respect for the tools of learning. Improper use of equipment sabotages projects and, ultimately, learning.

When breakdowns occur, students can become frustrated with the process of developing their projects, or they may lose essential time for the completion of their work. Even in well-run schools with properly functioning networks of hardware, wise teachers factor in time for malfunctions or delays based on hardware or software problems. The need to understand this aspect of technology is an important message for students as well. A smoothly running technological society depends upon smoothly running technology. When equipment malfunctions, the challenge of analyzing and solving the problems can provide important learning experiences.

Of course, prevention is the best solution to the problem of technical malfunctions. Where budgets are tight, schools tend to scrimp on maintenance. This is hardly cost-effective; the expense of repair usually outstrips the cost of maintenance by a considerable margin. A school tech aide might earn $10 an hour while computer repair people charge more than $50. Even when schools do not have support funds for a tech aide, it is still possible to train teachers in basic maintenance. Computers work best if they are used properly, if programs are opened and closed correctly, and if the correct startup and shutdown procedures are followed. Dust-free environments will protect equipment. It is always discouraging to see an expensive multimedia cart with an expensive AV computer and several optional peripherals parked next to the chalkboard and buried under a patina of grit. Scanning disks regularly for fragmentation or viruses is important. Automatic virus check programs are a must if students use disks that travel home or between machines at school. Lockout programs, which prevent student access to the station's and network's operation systems, prevent malfunction caused by curiosity or sabotage. (See pg. 73 for maintenance report form.)

Teacher cadres can be trained in basic maintenance and repairs. Local or regional technology programs regularly offer classes. While not as glamorous as multimedia training, this is crucial staff development, and administrators should take advantage of such opportunities. Teachers should be cautioned not to attempt major repair efforts, however, unless they have taken such a class. Well-meaning fiddling with a computer can lead to disaster. Ideally, a school has a tech aide who takes care of the daily maintenance of equipment and troubleshoots problems. A system for reporting problems and monitoring solutions should be in place. Once again, the digital world alters school job descriptions, from the custodial to the proactive.

Project Skills

Name _____ Pre-Test _____

Teacher _____ Post-Test _____

	Exceptional	Strong	Complete	Partially Complete	Minimally Complete	Needs Work
1. Accessing Information The student uses resources appropriate to research from a diverse spectrum of media.						
2. Processing Information The student interprets data in a meaningful way.						
3. Presenting Information The presentation is creative and original with appropriate use of visuals (time-lines, maps, pictures, etc.)						
3. Cooperative Learning The student facilitates the group in answering questions, solving problems, and overcoming obstacles						
	6	5	4	3	2	1

▶ COMPLETING THE CYCLE

As the student teams complete their research and construct the digital artifacts that will make up their multimedia presentations, the classroom teacher can continue the assessment process. The selection of material is critical, and evaluation should be based as much on what is left out as what is included. Student reflections, kept in daily logs or journals, can assist the teacher in understanding the processes that students used to create their final product. These logs are also valuable for evaluating the group process and surfacing problems within groups. Students may also record their own evaluation of the process and rate their final product in journals.

Once the construction of knowledge is finished, students may complete the process by producing a multimedia presentation. A wide variety of computer software now exists for such presentations, from simple slide show programs to Java-based authoring tools for professionals. The ability of young students to produce imaginative and informative multimedia presentations accounts for the popularity of such programs as *Kid Pix* by Broderbund and Roger Wagner's *HyperStudio*. Web-based projects, incorporating sound, graphics, video, animations, and Java script routines, represent an even higher level of presentation tools. Virtual reality projects, produced with *QuickTime* VR software or Autodesk 3D Studio VRML plug-ins, offer students the opportunity to "visit" their project in real time.

The finished productions become vehicles for further learning as they are presented to the learning community for appreciation and evaluation. Once again, computers have given the learning team a wide range of presentation options. Students may share each other's work offline through a classic "show and tell" around a single computer. Or they may browse each other's projects from the hard drives of individual machines in a lab. The teacher may choose to project the presentations with an LCD panel or projector or run the finished products onto videotape for dissemination to a wider audience. Web-based projects may find a home online on the local school Intranet, or they may find server space, which will take them out to the World Wide Web. Interactive projects of sufficient size can now be reproduced on inexpensive CD-ROMs. This range of presentation options affords unprecedented opportunity for students to learn from each other and from a wider audience who can participate in the process of evaluation and feedback.

▶ ELECTRONIC PORTFOLIOS

Ideally, assignments in the new learning environment are open-ended, and the cycle of inquiry does not end with a given project but spirals into a new dimension. But even when a project reaches a plateau and a variety of products have been created by students, it is important to understand the archival value of these productions. Properly archived multimedia can serve as learning tools for the next class of students. This system allows students to learn from the work of the preceding group and creates a baseline from which these new students will advance. Second, it allows students to see the quality of the work previously produced, and it challenges students to raise the standard of excellence. Third, as these archives are available to teachers, they may reduce plagiarism because these documents can be searched for common key words. More important, they serve as sample assignments on which to build increasingly challenging and creative activities. Creating permanent learning tools for succeeding classes is an important key to raising the standards in a given school.

Multimedia archives can also serve as electronic portfolios for student evaluation and for documentation of student progress. Commercial portfolio makers are now beginning to find their way onto the market. This archiving software allows the creation of individual portfolios on school servers, which students may access at anytime throughout their school career from any computer in the school. Thus, ongoing projects across disciplines or grade levels become easy to maintain and can easily be updated by students. Some of these systems even allow student access from home, and the students can build their own personal archive of information. From time to time, finished work is burned to CD-W, giving the students a permanent record of their work. The possible uses of such systems are wide-ranging and should be available for practical use in the next few years.

▶ MORE WORK FOR THE LEARNING TEAM

All of this means that the learning teams in schools have a great deal of homework to do in the foreseeable future. To be effective learning managers, they not only must master the cycle of inquiry and the cycle of production but also must stay abreast of all of the possible tools with which students will work. They must understand the need for hardware maintenance and the workings of the school server and network. They must move from being the sole evaluator of student effort to a part of a wider group of students, parents, and professionals who will take part in the assessment process. They must help educate not only their students but also the larger learning community about the changes taking place in education. This is not work that can be done by an individual on a given campus. It requires the effort of a team of trained professionals if it is going to succeed. Thus, teacher learning time also requires close examination and restructuring to ensure that staff can stay abreast of new technology.

Sample Equipment Program Report Form

Name: _____ Room: _____ Date: _____

Station number (if applicable): _____

Did you check the following:
Is the electricity working (outlet, switch, or power strip)?
Is it plugged in?
Are all the connections OK and secure?
Is it turned on?

For printers:
Is the paper tray filled?
Is there enough ink (toner, cartridge, or ribbon)?
Is the right printer selected on the computer system?

System questions:
Is the problem local to one machine?
Is the problem consistent or is it intermittent?
Does the problem exist for all software resources or just one?

Equipment:
Type of machine: _____ Brand: _____ Model: _____
Part of machine having trouble:

Description of problem:
When did it happen?
What happened at the time that the problem occurred?
What does the problem look like?
What did you do to correct the problem? What happened?
How urgent is the problem?

Action:
Date/time form received:
Who fixed the problem?   Date/time fixed:
Solution:

From *Training Student Library Staff*, p. 113.

Whose Work Is It Anyway?

How much knowledge is truly original? Isn't the idea of education to learn from those before you and add to that body of knowledge? Much of student research deals with uncovering other people's ideas and integrating them with one's own past experiences and beliefs. Analyzing the content of a source, in fact, recognizes the worthiness of that source and basically calls on students to interact with that material and make it their own. The source material is personalized, as it becomes one ingredient added to the rest of the person's mental ingredients to be stirred and kneaded into a new intellectual shape.

In the process, of course, that mental ingredient should be named and credited. What happens, though, when that source cannot be determined—when it has passed through several hands? To continue the cuisine analogy, think of a sourdough starter. It is passed from one person to another, and tracing its source can sometimes be problematic. With the advent of the Internet and its fluid trains of thought, tracing an idea worldwide can be an impossible task.

What is the basis of authorship? What grounds exist for intellectual property? Milton talked about the open market of ideas, but perhaps technology has made the world of ideas a communist state. Looking at the latest scramble of copyright efforts in the electronic age would indicate otherwise. Certainly, as projects and discovery learning embrace the digital world, these issue impact education as never before.

▶ REPURPOSING

Most teachers are acquainted with repurposing. They may extract scenes from a videotape or a recording to fit a particular lesson. English teachers routinely take a movie treatment of a novel or play and show sequences to make an instructional point. At its core, repurposing refers to analyzing an existing product created for one purpose and then selecting and reorganizing elements for another purpose.

Repurposing actually is at the heart of most research. Teachers and students find information intended for one objective and use it in another context. Just as one book can be used in several classes, so too can many non-print materials. Students learn how to transfer concepts from one course to another in the process. Unfortunately, technological products may be costly, so with limited budgets, schools can stretch their resources by repurposing. A *National Geographic* video may be used in both geography and science; a CD-ROM on American speeches can be used in history and English. Probably the greatest benefit of repurposing, though, is student repurposing. Using existing materials, students can put an original "spin" on the information and make it their own. In the process, they learn how to critically analyze content and implement the concepts of "point of view" and "audience."

Some media lend themselves more easily than others to repurposing. Slides have been used for decades in this manner; the same set of images can be sequenced in different ways to show themes, composition, chronology, or compare-contrast. While videotape might seem like a natural, without good equipment, it is cumbersome to locate specific frames. Most teachers don't have the time to cut out the desired sections and duplicate them in a new order onto another tape—and they may compromise copyright permissions in the process. This same access problem limits audiotapes.

With digital technology, access is much easier and more defined. Videodiscs, CDs, and CD-ROMs all have random-access capability to determine enter and out points. Sequencing and viewing excerpts can be as easy as jotting down desired frame numbers or key words, creating a log journal of entries, and presenting the new sequence by inputting the information. Hypermedia programs, such as *HyperStudio*, make it possible to input and organize the digital access points permanently. The "new" presentation can be viewed at any time. Additionally, hypermedia offers non-linear organization, so the creator can create decision points (e.g., menus and linked buttons) that allow users more control over the viewing sequence. In this way, a teacher might create a sophisticated HyperCard stack that serves as a highly-defined—albeit somewhat artificial—learning environment with which students can interact according to individual needs.

IMPROVISATION ON A THEME

Looking at a topic from different perspectives permits students to customize their learning. This time-honored approach to thematic learning acquires new life with the incorporation of technology. Even within one CD-ROM, different aspects can be explored. *Passage to Vietnam, Material World,* and *Frank Lloyd Wright* are three good examples of this multiple presentation. The first two focus on cultural geography and show different aspects of daily life as well as basic political facts. The Wright product shows styles, the architect's personal life, and even offers a virtual walk-through of three homes. Even sequential multimedia products, such as movies, or collections of items, such as a virtual art collection, may be repurposed within a single class according to student interest. For example, the *Musical Instruments* CD-ROM can be organized to show chronology of one or several instruments, geographic distribution of instruments, instruments of one county, a single type of instrument (e.g., percussion), instruments by tonal range, instruments by material (e.g., brass), or instruments by type of group (e.g., string quartet).

The strength of these more content-neutral resources is that they lend themselves to more manipulation and individualization by students. Students can express their own "voice" more powerfully by combining several sources or adding their own commentary to a single re-sequenced source. Students can customize further by choosing how to present their information—hypermedia stack, news magazine with captured images, simulated newscast with video clips from the source, or video constructed with computer-programmed selections. Thus, students have control of content, product, *and* process. Students also can learn firsthand about copyright laws and publishing ethics as they relate to this broad spectrum of information.

▸ WHO OWNS AN IDEA?

Intellectual property has been a controversial issue for years. The basic concept is to credit a person's original ideas, both intellectually and financially. The integrity of the work is the philosophical basis for legal decisions. Making money from other people's work or not paying for access to their work are the two economic reasons for copyright laws and punishments.

Regulations about print sources were updated in 1976 and are being reviewed to some extent now. Education usually comes under the fair use provision, which allows limited copying for research purposes, individually and in a classroom. The main factors are brevity (small percentage of content), spontaneity of use, and cumulative copying, so the same sources aren't repeatedly copied. It also should be noted that all copyright is not created equal. A publisher may have only first rights, with the author retaining the main rights. Some authors or publishers permit users to copy without permission under certain parameters. It always pays to check.

Non-print sources have much more complex regulations under fair use because they are usually viewed as a group, such as a performance. Four factors must be present for educational fair use:

▶ performed / played by teachers or students

▶ used in the course of face-to-face teaching

▶ shown in a non-profit instructional setting

▶ material must be legally acquired or copied.

Users must also follow guidelines specific to the publication type. A picture, for instance, isn't supposed to be enlarged, reduced, or cropped when copied. A taped television show can typically be held for 45 days, but students must see it during the first ten days. A software program can be archived but not used on more than one station at a time without permission. Backup copies of audiocassettes are not permitted. Music can be a special headache since the music itself, the recording, and the arrangement may each require separate permission. Even if the music is in the public domain, the arrangement or recording probably isn't. Once we venture into the electronic world, the laws can be extremely complicated and seemingly arbitrary. What about networking? What about downloading online databases for future use? What about scanning? What about closed-circuit TV or distance learning? The fact that electronic materials are sometimes patented instead of copyrighted makes the issue that much more confusing.

When students repurpose a source, copyright instantly comes into play. Certainly, students should credit their resource material in any case, but when they change a medium's sequencing, then the work is considered derivative, and different rules apply. The 1996 Fair Use Guidelines for Educational Media addresses the materials used for student- and teacher-produced derivative work. As long as the material complies with copy limits (which differ among media), a repurposed or derivative work may be shown to support direct instruction within the classroom or at a teacher conference within two years of creation without copyright permission. However, any distribution outside of that class of students requires permission, such as for a school open house or onto the Net. The message is this: use public domain or original work! These copyright issues more than ever underlie the importance of student synthesis of other information into a unique and original form of their own. Indeed, the possible publication of student work on the Internet means that the *educator* responsible must be well versed in copyright and laws and processes as well.

IS CODE THE SAME AS ATOMS?

Software programs are patented, not copyrighted, because they are considered to be inventions. The patent recognizes "any new and useful process, machine, manufacture, or compositions of matter, or any new and useful improvement thereof." (U.S. Patent and Trademark Office) The patent denies other people's right to make, use, or sell the invention without permission from the patent owner. However, an original work created with the software program, such as this book, would by copyrighted. The key is "form of expression." It should be noted that the significant incorporation of one computer program's code to create another software program would constitute a patent violation, especially if the *process* was being used for commercial gain.

Where does that put BASIC-generated programs or hypermedia authoring tools? In this case, the programming language holds the patent. For the program or stack to work, it has to be "played" using the original software program, so the financial security of the original inventors stays intact. The fact that the materials are electronic is not the issue; the main factor is the process/product.

TRACKING IDEAS

Back in traditional bibliography days, citing the originator of an idea could be complicated. If a source compiled information from another source, some acknowledgment of the original material needed to be made. Pictorial books cite an illustration's origin—usually in fine print in the back of the book. Part of this scrupulousness stems from the publisher, who has to make sure that proper credit is given to the original source and that proper permission is granted in order not to be sued for copyright infringement.

In the digital world, such copyright attention is not always displayed. The Software Publishers Association has been trying to strengthen this practice. However, many Web sites are not scrutinized by a careful editor or publisher. Graphics, in particular, often have no accompanying credit line. Not only is the originator being denied financial remuneration but also the viewer has no clue where to find the original work.

Of course, the Web master or file author may be contacted if that information is included in the document. Sometimes the authors have done sloppy research or adaptation themselves and have forgotten where the image originated. Like gossip or rumors, derivative Web pages can be a real hodgepodge of fifth- or sixth-generation text, images, and sounds.

What's a student to do? Make every effort to trace the work, which can result in a long line of search backs. Use authenticated sources. Check the credentials of the Web page author. Actually, this hunt for original ideas can be a fun experience, which can instill a genuine respect for creative ideas. It also can develop into an information web or network of ideas that defines the parameters of the intellectual inquiry to date. Professional researchers routinely trace ideas through a *literature review.* Now that process has metamorphosed into a multimedia global adventure.

Fortunately, today's search engines can facilitate the process. An amazing number of files are duplicated on servers throughout the world. Sometimes the title differs, but the content is the same—or nearly so. Search engines can list those duplications for the viewer to discriminate. With search engines geared specifically to images, students can use the source code to identify the image name, and then use that information to locate other files that incorporate the image. Hopefully, with this aid, students can find the original source.

▶ THE WEBLIOGRAPHY

The usual way to credit other people or sources is to compile a bibliography. More and more, web sites and telecommunication "conversations" are being cited alongside monographs and periodical articles, as well as multimedia resources. In other days, bibliographies were sometimes format-driven, so print items were separated from non-print ones. Nowadays, the emphasis is on the information content rather than its delivery.

A *Webliography* is an extension of the traditional bibliography. It may list all types of media sources, or it can simply be an annotated list of useful URLs. In a way, a printout of Net bookmarks can serve as a beginning Webliography. The strength of the Webliography, though, lies in the abstract or annotation about the source—a brief description of the content and arrangement. For instance, a site composed entirely of hyperlinks differs greatly from an electronic article. A company's description of its own products, such as recreational vehicles, will probably contradict a Ralph Nader report on those vehicles. The Webliography should be able to describe the sites well enough for the reader to differentiate among the sources.

A Webliography can serve as a good starting point for student research and projects. This electronic literature review helps students find the information gaps and further directs research. In some cases, a Webliography can be the final product for a research effort, or it can be a focus activity along a benchmark process.

A *narrative Webliography* provides a running commentary on sources covering a research topic. A typical sequence would be: 1) introduction; 2) background information or overview of web sites; 3) Web sites comprised of links to specific information; 4) series of specialized topics and accompanying Web sites (e.g., history, biography, geography, factors). Each section would be written in essay form to lead the user through the Web sites in an informed manner by describing each one and its application. As with the typical Webliography, the narrative Webliography can serve as an ersatz research report.

▶ BUILDING ON STUDENT FOUNDATIONS

One of the great benefits of in-depth student work is that it can be used as a foundation for future student work. For example, one class may develop a hypermedia stack on Jack London's *Call of the Wild.* Next year's class can interact with the stack at the beginning of the unit and can expand the stack either to deal with another London novel or to explore a parallel novel by another author, such as Bret Harte. The stack gains its own life while serving as a genuine model for student engagement and presentation.

Similarly, one class may create a videotape of a French skit. The following class can learn French from the first tape, and create its own drama video. Having set the bar for excellence, the first class poses an intellectual challenge for its successors. Students know that future classes will use their product as a basis for learning; the authentic audience serves as another impetus for high-quality work. In fact, with this kind of sequential competition, student work only gets better, and standards are raised naturally.

As a corollary, students should be taught that professional research, the way that civilizations expand knowledge, is conducted the same way. Today's medical advances build on yesterday's discoveries. Computers wouldn't be palm size if it weren't for the invention like the transistor. Airplanes can be traced back to Leonardo da Vinci's drawings. So, too, can student work lay the foundation for future classes. Doesn't this make much more sense than keeping a paper in the family closet—or the fraternity files?

Redwood HS Library: Webliography to World Problems 1998

❯ BACKGROUND INFORMATION

031	encyclopedias: under continent, country, subject (use index volume)
310	almanacs
910	atlases: world, regional, topical CD-ROMs: Encarta, Colliers, Grolier encyclopedias; Facts on File World Digest

❯ REFERENCE BOOKS

333.7	Statistical record of the environment
341.4	Amnesty International
355	New state of war and peace
909	Background notes (U.S. Department of State)
909.82	World today series (current information by continent, divided into countries)
909.83	Global studies (current information by continent, divided into countries)
910	Culturegrams

❯ INDEXES

National Geographic magazine
Reader's Guide to Periodical Literature
Magazine Articles Summaries (on CD-ROM)

❯ PAMPHLETS (BY COUNTRY)

❯ BOOKS

Look under the country, continent, topics

301.412	Women's issues
304.6	Population
305.4	Women's issues
305.8	Ethnic groups and relations
326	Migration
327	International relations
330	Economics
331	Labor
333.7	Ecology/Environment
341.7	International law
355	Military
361	Social problems and welfare
362.5	Homeless/poverty
363.3	Terrorism
364	Crime
370	Education

❯ WEB SITES

www.yahoo.com - look under Regional:countries
www.embpage.org - Embassy pages
www.emulateme.com - Profiles, flags around the world
flags.mmcolp.com/index.asp - Basic data about countries
ivory.nosc.mil/planet_earth/countries - Home pages for countries
www.odci.gov - CIA factbook about countries
lcweb2.loc.gov/frd.CS/Cshome.html#toc - Library of Congress info on countries
www.newslink.org - Periodicals from around the world
www.euromktg.com/euromktg/eurobus.html - European Business Center
www.igc.apc.org - Institute for Global communications (liberal bias)
www.imf.org - International Monetary Fund
worldculture.com - Various aspects of culture

CHAPTER 10

Where Are You in the Learning Curve?

Who is to say what shape education will take in the future? Education is in the forefront of the current political debate with good reason. The issues involved are staggering—from the huge cost of renovating obsolete physical plants nationwide to replacing an aging teaching force, and from redeveloping the curriculum to keep pace with our changing society and economy to developing and maintaining high academic standards that will guarantee America's place in the global information marketplace. Facilities may change radically, classrooms may morph into new forms never seen before, and the continuum of lifelong learning may transform adult-child relationships. Educators need to be prepared to experience change and to maintain a critical eye on the social and technical developments. They will be best prepared, however, if they can keep abreast of the digital revolution. The one certainty in all of this is that digital information systems will become primary in delivering the curriculum.

▶ MICROPOCKETS OF TECHNOLOGICAL POVERTY

Inequity in American education is not new. Books such as *Savage Inequalities* by Jonathan Kozol have detailed the plight of schools in America's inner cities and the tremendous difference between them and those in wealthy suburban districts. But the digital revolution is bringing with it a new form of inequity. Even in affluent neighborhoods, there exist clusters of students who are not being trained to understand digital technology.

There are many reasons why these micro pockets of technological poverty exist. Inner city schools may not be able to afford any technology, let alone staff development support. But even some affluent schools may feel that they do not need to develop a technology program for all students. Others may cluster their technology with a few "techie" teachers who can make the machines bow to their will, meaning that students not fortunate enough to take classes from those teachers never touch a computer. Many teachers ignore, or refuse to work with, new technologies. Frequently, the most able students are tracked into traditional book-oriented honors classes where teachers adopt a traditional approach to learning in the mistaken belief that this is what colleges want. Some parents may spend a fortune on the latest hardware for their children who, in turn, use it merely for video games and chat rooms. All of these reasons add up to large numbers of children who complete their education without even a rudimentary knowledge of digital information systems. The result is a huge bill delivered to the colleges and the workplace for training. The economic gap between the digital-savvy and ignorant can be devastating, and the solution, education, should be available equitably to all.

ADAPTING TO CHANGE

It is safe to say that no school in America—nor in the world—has yet implemented a learning system that fully uses technology as it will be used by most schools in the 21st century. The much-touted information superhighway does not extend to most schools, and even if it did, it is still under construction. While the current systems give us a general outline of what the future holds, each generation of hardware and each new advance in software alters the picture. Therefore, no one needs to apologize this year for not being current with these important trends. But in the coming years, it will be necessary to apologize deeply if a school has not kept pace with information technology. To appreciate the advance coming in the next five years, we must look back about ten years—before 300 megahertz processors, gigabyte storage, fiber backbone data transmission, and the World Wide Web. In the 1980s, new advances in hardware and software appeared about every three years. In 1998, a generation of software and hardware advances every 18 months. Entire systems become obsolete before they can be installed.

There actually are advantages for education to be behind the developmental technology curve. Some advances may be misleading fads, such as the 1960s "programmable" texts. Particularly since schools need to balance social stability and forward-thinking trends, educators need to examine bleeding-edge advances critically and build on the successes and failures of early adapters. The emphasis, though, needs to be on awareness of developments rather than on waiting for the "right" technology to come along. Otherwise, useful technology will bypass education—and needy students.

In order to keep pace, teachers will need to work together to understand the trends in technology as they appear on the horizon. No single teacher or media specialist at a school site can keep track of the changing digital landscape. Decisions that were once made by the "computer teacher" now require a team of committed professionals with the mindset to understand the new developments throughout their careers. The most important mindset of all, therefore, is the ability to adapt to change.

This is difficult for teachers, especially those who have been in the profession for more than ten years. Like many workers, they have spent those years refining systems that can be replicated—lectures, tests, favored texts, and a productive scope and sequence. To learn that these efforts may need to be scrapped to take advantage of an entirely new educational system is disconcerting to say the least. Many teachers have already adopted a "show me" attitude, refusing to accept the inevitable. While this has allowed them to remain comfortable temporarily, even the most resistant can feel the pressures building. Terminals take the place of the card catalog in the library media center. Students bring in word-processed reports that may be cut and paste jobs from the Internet or a CD-ROM encyclopedia. The administration does school business through e-mail rather than memos in staff mailboxes. Students ask if they can e-mail their homework. Others ask if they can submit a video production or a multimedia CD of their own manufacture instead of the standard term essay. School textbook adoptions include CD-ROM and laser disc materials. Districts give special salary credit to teachers with certificates in technology.

All of these pressures are representative of a revolution at the schoolhouse gates. As with many powerful revolutions, resistance only means a more violent end to the old regime. Teachers must realize what most successful business people now admit—that change is the norm. Thus, the first step on the learning curve is to maintain an adaptive attitude. Every school must develop systems to manage the change process. Tech committees, curriculum study groups, focus groups, and leadership teams must meet regularly and discuss trends in education and their application to each site's needs. All staff must stay informed as to the latest developments in educational hardware and software. Teachers must take advantage of opportunities to receive training in new technologies and teaching methods. Just as how to learn is as important as what to learn, how to teach becomes as essential as what to teach.

> UNDERSTANDING DIGITS

While many people can use a computer, most people have only a rudimentary understanding of how it works. This is in keeping with the general public's lack of understanding of most of our technological apparatus, from television sets and VCRs to automobiles. Generally speaking, our machines are transparent for us—as long as they work. When the television set functions properly, we are only in tune with the content; the medium and the apparatus that transports it are invisible. In the early days of television, consumers were more aware of the set as a machine. Tubes would malfunction and could be tested and replaced; colors had to be dialed in, sometimes several times an evening; and focus, contrast, and fine tuning were necessary every time viewers changed channels (which was done by turning knobs on the machine itself).

In the early days of personal computers, users were very much in tune with the machine since it required personal programming to work. Once commercial programs became available, the consumer began moving away from understanding the machine, and as computers become increasingly reliable, they become more like other household appliances. Users are only aware of them as machines when they fail to work. From a school point of view, of course, reliability is essential. But as educators, we must resist the tendency to forget how the machine operates if we are to be effective in using it as a tool.

To be effective, teachers and LMTs must keep certain basics in mind. First, computers are a digital medium. Information passes through them in digital sequences, no matter what the content. Everything else is predicated on this fact.

Understanding the computer's storage system and the way in which it manages files is the second basic. Electronic file management is an art, and it requires mastery to make full use of the medium. Creating documents and saving them on the hard drive or a floppy disk is just the beginning. Creating folders—for each class of students or even each assignment—and managing the contents is another step. Transferring files, either as downloads from the Internet or between hard drives on the school local area network, is another skill to be learned. Converting files through text or graphic converters in order to import and export them between programs is another level of understanding. Archiving files with compression software or the use of a mass storage device is yet another essential skill. There are many books available on file management, and teachers and LMTs should study them.

A third basic fact about computers is that, for the present at least, we can never learn enough. We are still in the trial and error stage of hardware and software development. Everything from operating systems and Internet browsers to software programs and multimedia components suffers from rapid development, a lack of clear cut standardization, and a plethora of incompatibilities, which makes working with the systems nerve wracking at times. This will undoubtedly smooth out, but not in the foreseeable future. Hopefully, the machines will be easier to use. But for the present time, every school will need several experts in operating systems, networking issues, and software manipulation. For obvious reasons, it is best if several staff members undertake this task.

▶ DIGITAL PUSH-UPS

Short of writing binary source code, it is hard to truly understand how the digital world works. Most of us only get to use these 1s and 0s on our computer desktop where they are already transformed into something more or less recognizable, such as a text or graphic or sound. Still, anyone who works with word processing software is already coming to terms with the plasticity of the binary code. Each time we cut and paste text, we are taking advantage of this marvelous quality. However, many people do not understand how important this quality is since they seldom combine media and usually work with only one application at a time. If you are just beginning to realize the power at your fingertips, here are some simple digital exercises.

Open a word processing document. Type for awhile. Alter the fonts, the spacing, the line length, and the document format using the various options in the format menus. Cut some text and paste it into another document. Open another program—a text editor or HTML editor—and paste the text into that program. Play around with it; the written word is no longer engraved in stone.

If your computer has enough memory, minimize your document and **open your paint program**. Scribble or draw. Select your drawing. Use the edit menu to copy your drawing. Reopen your document and paste the copy of your drawing into your document. (Use your program's online help if you have trouble.) A picture is worth a thousand bytes.

Learn the various graphics formats—.bmp, .pict, .jpeg, and .gif. Even Macintosh computers make these distinctions. Download a shareware graphics utility from the Internet. Practice converting a graphic from one format to another. Notice the different sizes in bytes as they convert from one format to another. Notice how the palettes may vary. Expand them, shrink them, crop them, and retouch them. They are just as pliable as words. Paste them into documents, Web pages, and HyperCard and HyperStudio stacks. Use them as e-mail postcards.

If you are not listening to music with your computer, you are missing out on a great deal of enjoyment. CD-quality sound is available in many formats. The Internet is now the world's greatest catalog of music, and much of it is free. A variety of media players exists; some come with your computer, and others are available on the Net.

Download a music MIDI file. If you have a standard multimedia computer with a MIDI mixer, reopen the file in the mixer program. See if you can cut and paste the selection into a new "non-linear" opus.

Video is just as digital as any other medium now. Even before DVD formats, digital video came in cut-and-paste formats like Quicktime and .AVI. Once again, your computer handles video with 1s and 0s just like it does words, pictures, or sounds. You can understand this best by playing with the medium. There are many non-linear editing programs on the market. They are easy to learn, mostly allowing you to cut-and-paste and drag-and-drop frames of video as if they were words. You can even combine sound tracks with them. People are producing movies entirely on the desktop of their computer. Hello, Hollywood!

These exercises will help you understand the power of the digital world. The secret is understanding that to the computer words, pictures, and sounds are made up of the same building blocks of code. Once you fully understand this, you will be better prepared for the digital future.

Educators as well as students can expect a lifetime of constant learning. Schools will need to develop strategies to adapt to new outside factors and improve educational practices to ensure that all students can succeed. All school personnel will need to understand that learning is part of the job and that keeping pace with technological advances is required. This can only be accomplished through collaboration within the school and within the broader learning community. In many instances, students will take the lead in developing the learning tools of the future.

Schools need to develop resources that will help them with the change process. A mindset that can see the entire range of issues and does not reduce the future to simplistic equations is the goal. The issue is not just technology or tools or computers. It is the modernization of every aspect of the learning system of the nation—from the configuration of the classroom to the assignments, from the media with which students access information and manipulate it to the assessment strategies employed—as well as the relationships between school personnel and students. In the next few years, every aspect of education will be affected. As technology advances, we can expect equal advances within the school environment. Managing these advances will be the task of the professional partners in learning of the digital world—classroom teachers and library media teachers.

Lessons Incorporating Technology

The following is a key to the structures of all the activities in the book.

ACTIVITY DESCRIPTION

a one-sentence general description of the activity.

CONTENT OUTCOMES

a list of student performances, products or knowledge related to a specific curriculum area.

INFORMATION LITERACY OUTCOMES

a list of student performances, products or knowledge related to the processing of information.

PRE-REQUISITE SKILLS

a list of those skills or concepts that the student should exhibit prior to beginning the activity. For example, if students are supposed to make a hypermedia product, then they should be able to create multimedia "screens" first.

RATIONALE FOR THE PROCESS

This section answers the question "Why are we doing this?" The issues and problems raised in this section are explored through the related activity.

ACTIVITY

Grade level: Identifies the general academic level for which the activity is geared.

Time frame: A general guideline for predicting the amount of time required to accomplish the entire activity. Daily periods of 45 to 60 minutes are assumed. The amount of time depends on the student's prior knowledge, the intent of the activity (whether for introducing new skills or reviewing old concepts), and the percentage of activity to be done outside of class time.

Resources: A general list of the types of resources that students will use to complete the activity.

Group tasks: The specific steps that students carry out independently.

Tips: This section guides educators as they facilitate group learning

Assessment: As much as possible, the criteria for evaluation should be given to the students at the beginning of the activity. Both individual and group work should be evaluated.

Activity variations: A list of possible ways to modify the content, skill, focus, groups, and presentation format.

Activity Title

ACTIVITY DESCRIPTION:

CONTENT OUTCOMES:
Students will:

INFORMATION LITERACY OUTCOMES:
Students will:

PRE-REQUISITE SKILLS:

RATIONALE FOR THE PROCESS:

ACTIVITY:

Grade level:

Time frame:

Resources:

Tasks:

Tips:

ASSESSMENT:

ACTIVITY VARIATIONS:

Mapping Rome

ACTIVITY DESCRIPTION:
Using Computer Assisted Design software, students create a series of maps detailing the expansion and collapse of the Roman Empire.

CONTENT OUTCOMES:
Students will:
- Identify the territorial conquests of the Roman army.
- Explain the difficulty of administering a vast empire from a central location.
- Identify external pressures on the Roman Empire caused by migrations of barbarian peoples.

INFORMATION LITERACY OUTCOMES:
Students will:
- Locate and select information about the Roman Empire.
- Use maps to analyze key concepts.
- Use geography-based software.
- Transform information into map form.

PRE-REQUISITE SKILLS:
- Use reference tools to access information about the Roman Empire's expansion and collapse.
- Draw electronically with a mouse and manipulate computer files.
- Use CAD software (optional).

RATIONALE FOR THE PROCESS:
Map study has long been a significant part of the social studies process. New CAD software makes the creation of detailed and accurate maps much easier for young students and speeds the process for them. Thus, students can create maps built around difficult concepts and can use them as visualization tools for important historical events. By creating a series of maps or map overlays, students can trace the process of conquest, the vastness of territory occupied by Rome, and the routes of various migrating peoples who created external pressures on the empire.

ACTIVITY:

Grade level: middle school and up

Time frame: five to six days (three computer lab days)

Resources: text and map resources on the Roman Empire, Internet access, CAD software.

Tasks:

1. Identify and choose one region of the classical world occupied by Rome.

2. Determine dates of Roman expansion and invasion.

3. Locate various provinces and capitals and routes required for logistical support.

4. Trace routes of migrating peoples and dates of their advance into the Empire.

5. Using CAD software, or a good precision drawing program; create maps and keys to detail these events.

Tips: Some CAD software allows students to use layering techniques, which allow the creation of templates to show different social, political, and military concepts on the same outline set. These can be printed on transparencies in different colors and projected with overhead projector for student presentations. To be most effective, the maps should all be drawn to the same scale.

ASSESSMENT:

Students present their maps as part of a general discussion on Roman politics and use the data for evidence. Assessment should be based on accuracy of data and precision in rendering. The class then discusses the challenges of Roman rule and the impact of neighboring peoples.

ACTIVITY VARIATIONS:

1. Animate the above concepts using computer animation software.

2. Create hot-linked hypermedia-based maps with pop-up dialog boxes about the events.

Exploring Islam

ACTIVITY DESCRIPTION:
Students design a Web-based multimedia report about an aspect of Islam.

CONTENT OUTCOMES:
Students will:
- Investigate in depth a major scientific concept or social studies aspect of Islam.
- Work cooperatively to identify key concepts of Islam.
- Identify the religious, historical and cultural impacts of Islam.

INFORMATION LITERACY OUTCOMES:
Students will:
- Pose essential questions about their topic.
- Use a variety of resources to gather information about their questions.
- Analyze the information and identify key concepts.
- Choose appropriate media for demonstration of knowledge.
- Design a multimedia Web site to convey their information to a wider audience.

PRE-REQUISITE SKILLS:
- Use reference tools to access information about Islam.
- Ability to synthesize essential information from notes.
- Develop Web pages (optional).

RATIONALE FOR THE PROCESS:
While Islam as a formal religion dates back to the seventh century, its impact has become obvious in the late twentieth century. By gaining an historical perspective of this religion, students will better understand its religious influence, historical force, and socio-cultural presence.

ACTIVITY:
Grade level: middle school up
Time frame: four to six days
Resources: sources about Islam and related topics, Internet access, web authoring software.
GroupTasks:

1. Choose a key area of Islam.
2. Research the key area using a variety of resources.
3. Organize findings into Web page design.
4. Create a Web page on the key area.

Tips: Begin the study by having students create K-W-L charts, listing what they Know, what they Want to know, and ways to Learn about Islam. Educate students on various branches of Islam and differences among them. The teacher or the class divides the study of Islam into key areas, such as:
- The Rise of Muhammad
- The Five Pillars of Islam
- The Spread of the Religion
- Major Dynasties

Islamic Science and Culture
Islamic Spain

Students should be encouraged to use a variety of sources, including print, Internet, CD-ROM, videotape, and discussions with members of the Islamic faith (either in person or online). To facilitate online work, bookmark key Web sites in advance.

Students should determine their group role before exploring the major area. Tasks for each team include researchers, web designers, graphic artists, writers, and editors. As students develop information, it can be re-deployed in hypertext format, using web pages as an authoring system. To standardize the Web page's appearance, have the class design a hypertext template with paper and pencil before rendering information in electronic form.

ASSESSMENT:

Rubrics developed by the class in concert with the teacher are best for this activity. Key factors should include depth of research, clarity of information, and quality of web design. Peers assess the Web pages according to the rubric. A class discussion can tie historical Islamic aspects to its modern-day influence.

ACTIVITY VARIATIONS:

1. Create video presentations of the information.

2. Study Islam according to country.

3. Develop a spreadsheet about Islam through history.

4. Study other religions.

HISTORY OF ISLAM CD

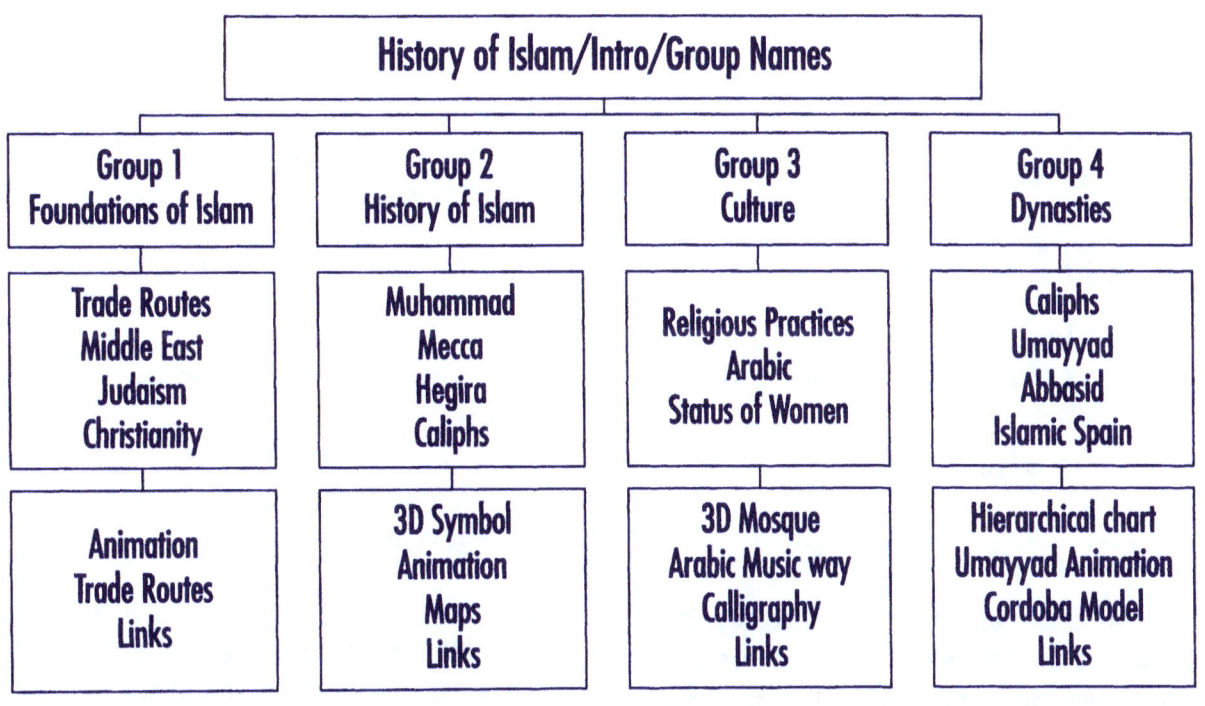

Castles and Cathedrals

ACTIVITY DESCRIPTION:
Students use computer-aided design software to create architectural styles and forms of the Middle Ages.

CONTENT OUTCOMES:

Students will:

▶ Relate form and function to architecture.

▶ Identify medieval architectural forms.

▶ Explain the role of social and cultural factors in determining architectural styles.

▶ Analyze modern architectural forms and functions in comparison to medieval architecture.

INFORMATION LITERACY OUTCOMES:

Students will:

▶ Use reference tools, including online sources, to access information about medieval architecture.

▶ Use content analysis to determine relationships between form and function.

▶ Use CAD software to demonstrate architectural concepts.

PRE-REQUISITE SKILLS:

▶ Ability to perform computer skills—conduct a simple Internet search, draw, manipulate files.

▶ Use CAD software (optional).

RATIONALE FOR THE PROCESS:

While medieval architecture, especially the castle and the cathedral, has been distorted in children's minds through overly romantic portrayals in movies, cartoons, and children's historical fiction, a true understanding of these classic forms allows students to gain critical insights into the true purposes of major architectural archetypes. In addition, this study helps students understand the role of social hierarchies and customs in determining architectural forms.

ACTIVITY:

Grade level: middle school and up

Time frame: four to five days

Resources: sources about the Middle Ages and architecture (Macaulay's *Castle* and *Cathedral* recommended), Internet access, CAD software and accompanying workstations

Tasks:

1 Research medieval architecture—forms and functions.

2 Choose one aspect of medieval architecture.

3 Identify critical features of the architecture.

4 Design an original structure using the architectural features.

5 Explain how form and function work together in modern architectural forms, such as skyscrapers and public buildings.

Tips: While studying the Middle Ages, students are introduced to the concepts of form and function in architecture. Sharing Macaulay's work, either through book or video, helps concretize medieval building. To further understand these factors, lead a class discussion about architecture by asking questions such as:

- What is the function of a fort? a moat? a tower?
- How does the material used in a building influence its use?
- How does the location of a building influence its use?
- How would a building imply social status?

Students may need help focusing on one architectural issue. They should be encouraged to choose one time period, one architectural form (e.g., cathedral, castle, hut), or function (e.g., defense, worship, storage). However, students should be encouraged to show at least two variations on their topic to facilitate identifying critical features. Thus, one group might contrast a Byzantine and a Romanesque basilica.

Students may choose to complete graphic renderings, animations, or 3D models to demonstrate their understanding of the basic elements of these structures. Cooperative groups may be used to divide the work. Each group also may choose a different architectural style or form.

ASSESSMENT:

Peers assess the renderings in terms of function, design, and historical correctness. As a class, students identify the critical features of each structure. Peers also assess the oral explanations about form and function in modern architectural forms in terms of justification and thoroughness. A good closing activity is to use the Frank Lloyd Wright CD-ROM to reinforce the concepts of form and function in modern architecture.

ACTIVITY VARIATIONS:

1. Choose another time period.

2. Compare architecture in different cultures during the same time period.

3. Broaden or narrow the means to render the structure.

4. Develop a Web page or slide show about architectural form and function.

Freewheeling Vertices

ACTIVITY DESCRIPTION:
Students study properties of triangles by manipulating vertices with CAD or math software.

CONTENT OUTCOMES:
Students will:
- Identify components of triangles, such as base, sides, vertices, perimeter, area, and angle.
- Use precision drawing programs to study geometry.

INFORMATION LITERACY OUTCOMES:
Students will:
- Manipulate CAD software to discover mathematical patterns.
- Use computer techniques—manage files, use mouse techniques, practice screen skills.

PRE-REQUISITE SKILLS:
- Basic computer skills—use keyboard, draw with a mouse, save a file.

RATIONALE FOR THE PROCESS:
Students who learn geometry using pencil and paper have limited experience due to the time consumed through the creation of basic geometric primitives. Precision drawing programs of the CAD variety or specialized geometry software allows the rapid creation and manipulation of a variety of basic shapes and allows students to gain a conceptual understanding of the dynamics of polygons.

ACTIVITY:

Grade level: middle school and up

Time frame: two to three days

Resources: CAD (computer-aided design) software

Tasks:

1. Create a triangle using a CAD program.
2. Calculate the triangle's dimensions, angles, and area.
3. Alter the elements of the triangle by dragging a vertex vertically or horizontally.
4. Calculate the new dimensions, angles, and area, observing the changes in each.
4. Create a new triangle by dragging the top vertex horizontally, so that the base and height remain the same.
5. Do Number 4 again, and verify the universality of the formula for area.

Tips: Have students take advantage of the software's measurement functions. To facilitate comparisons, remind students to copy and save their triangles. A grid can help students fix the base of their new triangles.

ASSESSMENT:

Students write a brief description of their experiments with triangles, and draw conclusions based on their observations. Accuracy and depth of insights form the basis for the assessment process.

ACTIVITY VARIATIONS:

1. Insert and drag vertices into lines to create new polygons from existing shapes.

2. Develop formulae for measurement of perimeter based on manipulation and calculation of primitives.

Supply and Demand

ACTIVITY DESCRIPTION:
Students create an animation illustrating the laws of supply and demand.

CONTENT OUTCOMES:

Students will:

▶ Identify the basic laws of supply and demand.

▶ Demonstrate how factors govern these laws.

INFORMATION LITERACY OUTCOMES:

Students will:

▶ Collect data on supply and demand from a variety of resources.

▶ Manipulate data through spreadsheets and graphs.

▶ Transform supply and demand content into animation form.

PRE-REQUISITE SKILLS:

▶ Read and interpret basic graphical information.

▶ Draw with a mouse.

RATIONALE FOR THE PROCESS:

Much of economics is best understood visually, particularly through spreadsheets, graphs, and charts. However, because most concepts are dynamic, static textbook diagrams lack the necessary vitality for true understanding. By animating examples of economic principles—the change in demand for automobiles from 1920 to 1990 or the curve in the demands for CDs over vinyl records from 1978 to the present—students gain a sense of the dynamics of economics.

ACTIVITY:

Grade level: middle school and up

Time frame: six to eight days

Resources: economic information, supply and demand information about products, Internet access, animation program, storyboard supplies

Tasks:

1 Choose a commodity to supply in terms of supply and demand.

2 Gather data about the commodity's quantity and pricing over a period of time.

3 Determine the changes in supply and demand of the given goods. Research possible factors affecting changes.

4 Storyboard an animation demonstrating the changes in supply and demand and the factors affecting change.

5 Using animation software, create an animation exemplifying the main aspects of the chosen topic.

Tips: To help students begin the project, have the entire class compare the impact of supply and demand.

Provide a couple of examples of how the factors affect one

another.

One factor that may be misleading is cost. Discuss with students the concept of a price index. Students may need to recalculate figures in terms of a standard price index; alternatively, graphs may show actual costs irrespective of the price index. However, one standard must be used across the board.

To facilitate the process, students may work in pairs, with one student concentrating on supply and one on demand for the same commodity. In that way, students can share research on factors that affect either supply or demand.

To help students visualize an animation, brainstorm with the class about the elements of movement. How could supply and demand be shown in this manner? Note that some students may have no experience in creating animations. As much as possible, pair non-users with users to encourage peer coaching. If the class as a whole is not used to animation software, then the project will take more time since instructional time needs to be devoted to learning the software.

ASSESSMENT:

Student work is evaluated by peers according to a rubric that includes animation technique and economic understanding. Students may help design the rubric. Information should be accurate and thorough, and the interaction between supply and demand should be evident.

Afterward, the class discusses the patterns among the commodities and time frames.

ACTIVITY VARIATIONS:

1. Choose one time frame for the entire class; compare commodity supply and demand.

2. Compare U.S. and foreign supply and demand.

3. Research how different forms of government (e.g., communism, socialism, fascism) affect supply and demand.

4. Use transparencies instead of animation to demonstrate supply and demand.

Growing Up in Time

ACTIVITY DESCRIPTION:
Each group produces a Web page about being a child or young adult during a period in American history.

CONTENT OUTCOMES:

Students will:

▶ Identify major characteristics of an American historical period (events, daily life, politics, and demographics).

▶ Accurately describe the conditions of being a child or young adult during an American historical period.

▶ Compare conditions between age groups and historical periods.

INFORMATION LITERACY OUTCOMES:

Students will:

▶ Recognize and use a variety of sources, especially primary sources, of information about youth in specific periods of American history.

▶ Assess information from a variety of sources to verify facts, recognize perspectives, and determine adequacy of information.

▶ Synthesize and organize findings into web page format.

PRE-REQUISITE SKILLS:

▶ Use reference tools to access sources.

▶ Create a Web page (optional).

RATIONALE FOR THE PROCESS:

Growing up is an immediate issue for youth. Comparing today's conditions with those of other historical periods in America helps students learn to crystallize and humanize facts. By creating Web pages, students share their findings with their counterparts and learn from each other.

ACTIVITY:

Grade level: middle school and up

Time frame: ten days

Resources: Library of Congress on-line American Memory collection; other online primary sources (e.g., UC Berkeley's digital library, University of Virginia's primary sources), *American Heritage* articles, monographs of each period, local history collections. Web authoring tools, scanners, DTP.

Grouping: small heterogeneous cooperative groups; middle school students will research being a child while high school students will research being a young adult.

Group tasks:

1. Choose a period in American history.

2. Locate and select information, especially primary sources, about being a child or young adult during that period.

3 Determine one demographic feature; i.e., one socioeconomic situation or region, for each student to use to focus and differentiate his research.

4 Based on the analysis of information, publish a visual and textual description of the youths' conditions or situations on a Web page.

5 High school students will compare the conditions or situations of children and young adults, based on the middle and high school Web pages.

Tips: Introduce the activity by leading a class discussion about growing up now, asking questions such as:
- What distinguishes today's youth?
- What issues do youth have to deal with?
- How does the socioeconomic condition influence growing up?
- How might the historical period affect youth development?

Remind groups to search for information from various angles—by ethnic groups, by time, by region, by social topic (e.g., gender roles, family, daily life). Explain how details can make the description more effective by discussing a typical day and its factors—food, transportation, clothing, home life, and money. This will help students ferret out interesting aspects of the period.

Groups should also use a variety of information formats—eyewitness accounts, film documentaries, oral histories, and illustrations.

ASSESSMENT:

Each group publishes a Web page, which is evaluated by its partner school counterparts. Criteria will include accuracy, thoroughness, appearance, and technical skill. Classes discuss growing up in different historical periods, comparing socioeconomic conditions as well.

ACTIVITY VARIATIONS:

1 Choose a different culture.

2 Use only primary documents.

3 Create a videotaped simulation.

4 Limit the class to one time period, and research lifestyles for people of different ages.

Archetypal Videos

ACTIVITY DESCRIPTION:
Each group creates a videotape of archetypal characters.

CONTENT OUTCOMES:
Students will:
- Identify character archetypes.
- Identify key elements within a video that exemplify a character archetype.
- Match video selections with a character archetype.

INFORMATION LITERACY OUTCOMES:
- Select and evaluate videotapes that exemplify a character archetype.
- Use content analysis to identify archetypes in video.
- Edit video selections into a synthesized videotape.

PRE-REQUISITE SKILLS:
- Use reference tools to access information about movie characters and archetypes.
- Edit a videotape (optional).

RATIONALE FOR THE PROCESS:
Character archetypes are used throughout literature and the media. They help the reader or viewer identify with the product as well as personalize universal conflicts. By using video versions of films or television selections, students can draw parallels between their reading and visual elements. In addition, content analysis of visuals helps students learn about critical features distinguishing an archetype.

ACTIVITY:
Grade level: high school
Time frame: six to eight days
Resources: sources about archetypes and movies, video player, video editing equipment or camcorder

Group tasks:
1. Choose a character archetype.
2. Research elements of the archetype.
3. Locate videos (probably of movies) that exemplify the archetype.
4. Select video clips that exemplify the archetype.
5. Create a videotape of the sequenced video clips.

Tips: Start the activity by talking about character archetypes. Have students brainstorm a list of archetypes (e.g., bully, wallflower, optimist, and clown). Then have them identify cartoon or TV characters that exemplify such archetypes. Discuss what visual clues help the viewer identify the archetype. Ideally, the character archetypes should link with classroom reading.

To help students locate movies that show archetypes, have

students link movie genres with archetypes. Also, as each group chooses an archetype, the information can be posted so other groups can suggest feasible movies. Students may also choose television programs to exemplify archetypes; sit-coms are especially fruitful sources.

Some of this work will need to be done at home since schools have limited video equipment. Students without home equipment should have first preference for school equipment use. Each person can choose one video to watch and select video clips.

Since video editing equipment is usually scarce, students should be taught how to use a camcorder to edit video:

1. Key each video selection so the clip will start in about 10 seconds.
2. "Black" a blank videotape by recording it with the camcorder lens on in a quiet room. This helps prevent static between the video clips.
3. Connect the camcorder to the VCR with the video/audio OUT from the camera and the video/audio into the VCR.
4. Start the blacked videotape in the VCR. After about 30 seconds, press "pause."
5. Start the first video clip in the camcorder. When the selection starts, press the "record-play" button on the VCR. Press the VCR "pause" when the video clip is done.
6. Press the camcorder "stop" button.
7. Repeat steps 5 and 6 until finished.

Students may need parameters for the videotape. To help students concentrate on critical elements, it is better to have a shorter tape with several short clips than a long tape with one or two long clips. A good guideline is three to five minutes with at least two clips from each video (one per group member).

ASSESSMENT:

Groups present their videotapes, and peers guess what character archetype is being exemplified. Groups should also give a brief presentation about their process of selection. Assessment is based on the appropriateness of the video selections.

The class as a whole discusses character archetypes and relates them to literary works.

ACTIVITY VARIATIONS:

1 Choose artwork that exemplifies character archetypes.

2 Each group picks one video or film, identifying character archetypes within it.

Morphing Artists

ACTIVITY DESCRIPTION:
Each student morphs two pieces of artwork to analyze style and composition.

CONTENT OUTCOMES:
Students will:
- Identify artistic styles.
- Distinguish between size and proportion.
- Label artwork according to art terms.
- Compare and contrast artistic styles and compositions.

INFORMATION LITERACY OUTCOMES:
Students will:
- Locate and select visual examples of artistic styles.
- Metamorphose artwork using a computer graphics program.
- Use content analysis to assess artistic styles or compositions.

PRE-REQUISITE SKILLS:
- Use reference tools to access artistic works.
- Use a computer graphics (morphing) program (optional).

RATIONALE FOR THE PROCESS:
Many artists choose similar subjects to illustrate, but their treatments may vary enormously. Even two portraits of the same person can differ significantly. How can you identify a Van Gogh painting? What makes a Dali a Dali? Each artist has distinguishing features. Not that style is written—or painted—in stone. Consider Picasso's changing style. However, some unique qualities still apply. One way to facilitate comparisons between one artist's works or to distinguish one artist from another is through metamorphosis. As one picture blends into another, the stable and changing features become more obvious. A computer morphing program provides an easy, fun way to accomplish such visual content analysis.

ACTIVITY:
Grade level: high school

Time frame: five days (more time if learning the morphing program)

Resources: sources of artwork (books, picture files, CD-ROM, laser disk, Internet), computer morphing program and scanner

Tasks:

1. Identify one or two artists.

2. Locate and select two pieces of artwork. The two compositions should be similar to expedite morphing. The styles may differ as may the artists.

3. Scan each piece of artwork into the computer, and use a morphing program to change from the first to the second artwork. Ideally, print stages of the metamorphosis (start, 1/4 change, 1/2 change, 3/4 change, end).

4 Using the prints as a guide, compare the two artworks.

Tips: To help students visualize the project, begin by sharing derivative works of *American Gothic* or the Mona Lisa. Have the class identify what artistic elements are shared by the "copies" and what features distinguish them. Some of the factors should include medium, color, degree of detail, proportion, texture, and line. Then share two similar compositions, such as portraits, by the same artists, repeating the content analysis of the artworks.

To help students find feasible art examples, encourage them to consult thematic art sources (e.g., angels, horses). They may find suitable pictures using Internet image search engines, such as isurf.yahoo.com, or accessing museum sources (CD-ROM, laser disk, online).

Because it is easier to morph images of similar composition (i.e., same size head, similar placement of objects on a page), students should choose their artwork carefully. On the other hand, if one art piece is much larger than another, the differences can be accommodated by resizing a scanned image.

Remind students to watch those elements that change and those that remain the same throughout the morphing process. These factors help constitute the critical features on which to compare artwork.

ASSESSMENT:

Descriptions and images are separated. Using the description, peers identify the artwork. They then assess the description in terms of critical analysis, use of art terms, and general accuracy.

The class discusses critical artistic features and generic content analysis of artwork.

ACTIVITY VARIATIONS:

1 Compare to photographs.

2 Compare a photograph and a painting.

3 Using a computer graphics program, create a piece of artwork in an artist's style, using a different composition.

Safe Science

ACTIVITY DESCRIPTION:
Each group produces a hypermedia stack on a science experiment.

CONTENT OUTCOMES:
Students will:
- Develop a science experiment.
- Identify and follow scientific processes.
- Determine independent and dependent variables.
- Make accurate predictions about cause and effect relationships.
- Create accurate equations to explain chemical reactions.

INFORMATION LITERACY OUTCOMES:
Students will:
- Locate and select information about science experiments, including chemical reactions.
- Develop decision flow charts about scientific processes.
- Transform a scientific experiment into hypermedia format.

PRE-REQUISITE SKILLS:
- Use the scientific method.
- Create a flow chart of decision chart (optional).
- Produce a hypermedia stack (optional).

RATIONALE FOR THE PROCESS:
Science experiments are fun to do, but often there's not enough time or material for everyone to truly explore the consequences of changing variables. Moreover, some science experiments are not safe or feasible to do in class. This project enables students to predict the outcomes of science decisions in an interactive, visual manner. It also helps them demonstrate clear science procedures.

ACTIVITY:

Grade level: high school

Time frame: five to six days, including experiment (more time if learning authoring program)

Resources: science experiment materials, sources on science experiments and processes, hypermedia authoring program

Group tasks:

1. Choose a science experiment or procedure.

2. Identify the independent and dependent variables.

3. Research the cause-effect relationships through direct experimentation, equation manipulation, or indirect information (reports, studies).

4. Change the variables and predict or determine the outcome.

5. Create a hypermedia stack that shows the results of each change. Design in such a way that each step involves a decision.

Tips: To help students clarify their tasks, walk through an existing science experiment, determining the variables and decision points. Have the class draw a decision flow chart to visualize the experiment and its variations. Students may use a "what-if" model to stimulate ideas.

Students may need help finding information about science experiments. They can find current magazine articles and science Web sites. "Ask a Scientist" options provide a personal touch for some students. Students should also be encouraged to find broader information and then transfer the concepts to their experiment. In some cases, students may want to start with a chemical equation and work backward from the abstract to the physical.

If students do not know how to create a hypermedia stack, then additional time is needed. (The project should be accomplished in a week or so if students are proficient in presentation authoring tools.) If some students can produce a stack technically, then they can be members in different groups and act as the layout expert. In that way, peers can explain what they want to accomplish, and the layout expert can translate the information into stack format without committing significant extra time to the project. Students should be encouraged, however, to shadow the expert, so they eventually can learn this technical skill.

ASSESSMENT:

Peer groups test the science experiments, following the decision links to see what happens. They assess the stacks for accuracy, thoroughness, technical quality, and appearance. As an assessment activity linked to the original project, students can compare their projects with their peers'.

As a class, students draw conclusions about science experiments, categorizing them by types of reactions, equations, and so forth.

ACTIVITY VARIATIONS:

1. Create equations and then develop experiments to test the equations.

2. Limit the type of experiment to one topic in science.

3. Have each group develop an experiment that deals with a different type of science.

Water Survey

ACTIVITY DESCRIPTION:
Each group surveys a different state in terms of water usage and displays its findings in graph or visual form.

CONTENT OUTCOMES:
Students will:
- Identify different uses of water.
- Convert water usage into comparable energy units.
- Assess water usage on a geographic basis.
- Draw inferences about factors that contribute to water usage.

INFORMATION LITERACY OUTCOMES:
Students will:
- Recognize and use a variety of sources to locate information about water usage.
- Intercept and use graph and tabular representations of information.
- Interpret data by recognizing cause-and-effect relationships.
- Organize information using statistical and graphing techniques.

PRE-REQUISITE SKILLS:
- Use library catalogs and indexes to locate information.
- Use survey techniques.
- Use basic statistical techniques.

RATIONALE FOR THE PROCESS:
Water is a resource for life, yet students often do not realize the many forms that water resources take. State figures provide more manageable numbers for comparison, and they illustrate the different patterns of usage due to local needs, resources, and climate. These figures may be translated into various charts and comparative methods, which simplify understanding and analysis while illustrating a variety of statistical techniques. In addition, students can start asking questions about water usage and its impact on state and interstate economics, politics, and environment issues.

ACTIVITY:

Grade level: high school
Time frame: two to four days
Resources: almanacs, encyclopedias, specialized reference sources on states, and water use resources on statistics and graphs

Group tasks:

1. Identify different forms of water use.
2. Locate and select information about water use, specifically by state.
3. Translate figures into comparable energy units.
4. Translate figures into graph format, e.g., a pie chart or bar graph.
5. Assess comparative water usage, drawing inferences about cause-and-effect relationships.
6. Assess water usage across geographic lines.

Tips: Students need to be conscious of different sources on water usage, statistical data, and the importance of timely information. They can look in geography and geology sources, electricity or other energy information, environmental impact reports and local water plans, as well as resources on water. Students may not be aware of specialized statistical sources, such as environmental or energy databases.

Translating figures into graph form may be difficult for some students. They may need to locate models or similar examples. Remind students that many formats may describe the same data; show some examples.

As groups assess their data, they will need to have a common ground for comparison—that is, comparable energy units. If groups assess their findings relative to the other groups' findings, then standardized graph formats as well as comparable energy units must be used.

Furthermore, students need to assess energy usage in light of factors beyond energy units. Lead a brainstorming session on contributing factors, asking open-ended questions such as:

- How would population affect energy usage?
- How would geographic size or location affect energy usage?
- How would available national resources affect energy usage?
- How would industry affect energy usage?

Groups then may conduct further research to provide more meaningful comparisons and inferences. This additional portion of the activity may require two to three days of work and processing.

ASSESSMENT:

Each group presents its findings in graph format. Group pairs may exchange graphs and compare their assessments.

As another assessment activity, new teams may be formed from members of each original group. The new teams each focus on one form of energy, comparing usage across geographic regions.

As a closing assessment activity, the class discusses energy usage and contributing factors to differences.

ACTIVITY VARIATIONS:

1. The entire class may concentrate on the same figures. Each group describes the data in different graph format.

2. The entire class may concentrate on one region of the world and subdivide energy usage by state or other political or geographic area.

3. The entire class may develop a database on energy usage rather than a graph presentation. If an integrated computer program is used, graph representations may be computer-generated.

4. The entire class may concentrate on one graph format, such as the bar graph.

5. Each group may assess energy usage by comparing forms or energy either within a state or across states.

6. Different statistical units may be used, such as per-capita use or square mile usage, as well as per-minute usage.

Food on the Run

ACTIVITY DESCRIPTION:
Each group creates an animated map of food migrations over time.

CONTENT OUTCOMES:
Students will:
- Identify patterns of food migration.
- Identify cause-effect relationships between foods and civilization.

INFORMATION LITERACY OUTCOMES:
Students will:
- Locate information about food migration.
- Transform information into hypermedia format.

PRE-REQUISITE SKILLS:
- Use reference tools to access musical and visual sources.
- Use an animation or hypermedia program.

RATIONALE FOR THE PROCESS:
The old adage "An army marches on its stomach" reflects the strong influence that food has on civilization. After all, it was agriculture that transformed nomads into stable residents who would build cities. With exploration, foods were transported to new lands, and the people followed. By creating animated maps of food migrations, chiefly by human means, students can gain insight into the social affect that food has.

ACTIVITY:
Grade level: high school
Time frame: five days
Resources: resources on food and civilization, maps, hypermedia animation program

Group tasks:

1. Select one food to trace.

2. Trace food migration over time, noting cause-effect relationships.

3. Develop a time line with facts about the food and its role in civilization.

4. Create a computer-animated map that shows the migration of food and its influence.

Tips: To focus students, discuss present-day foods and their origins. Students can look at food labels to see where foods have been imported—bananas from Ecuador, grapes from Chile, dates from Greece. Mention how foods have been transported over time, like the potato, which originally came from South America. Mention that the introduction of food can influence people's lifestyles because of new ways of agriculture or even new plant diseases.

Students may have a hard time finding the direct correlation of food to culture. Brainstorm with them ways that culture or civilization could be affected by food. Some factors should include:
- blights or other plant diseases
- famines
- new industries or fields of employment
- religious observances
- preservation influences.

ASSESSMENT:

Peers present their animated programs to be assessed for accuracy, thoroughness, and technical skill. The class as a whole makes generalizations about food migrations and cultural impact.

ACTIVITY VARIATIONS:

1. Trace other migrations, such as languages and religions.

2. Use transparencies to show the food migration.

3. Create a hot-linked map to show the distribution of food or cross-cultural food "genres" such as meat pies, raw fish, and pancakes.

More Idea Starters

FINE ARTS:

- Virtual tours of art themes
- Artist timelines
- CAD-generated fashion
- Hypermedia stack on schools of art
- Database of musicians
- Scientific probes to measure the physics of musical instruments

HEALTH AND FITNESS:

- Statistical inferences from *Sports Illustrated Almanac*
- Web page about disabilities
- Physical fitness diagnosis using scientific measurement instruments
- Animation about sports physics
- Calorie analysis using graphing calculators
- Database of exercises

LANGUAGE ARTS:

- Content analysis of videotaped speeches
- Student-produced photo novellas in foreign languages
- Virtual author visits
- Mock TV advertisements for persuasive arguments
- Claymation short story
- Foreign culture brochures

MATHEMATICS:

- Plotting economic trends with graphing calculators
- Photos of geometry in nature
- Videotaping of math in the work place
- Hot-linked map of mathematical history

SCIENCE:

- Technical cross-sections through transparencies or hypermedia
- Database of vitamins and minerals
- CAD-generated comparative anatomy
- Hypermedia stack about the brain and how it works
- Biome metamorphosis
- Hot-linked map of endangered species
- Bridge construction using Interactive *Physics* software
- Hypermedia cell division
- Database of plants
- Water sampling and analysis using scientific probes
- Videotape of everyday physics

SOCIAL STUDIES:

- Hypermedia stack about war decisions
- Hypermedia stack about the historic treatment of the mentally ill
- CAD-generated utopias
- Simulated news casts in history (i.e., TV's *You Were There*)
- Simulated newspapers of historical events
- Virtual panel discussion among philosophers
- Multimedia dating game
- Video oral histories
- Analyzing film treatments of history
- Web pages for local groups
- Video yearbook of school life
- Audiotape of school alumni histories
- Hypermedia stack on political campaigns

VOCATIONAL GUIDANCE:

- Video job shadowing
- Analysis of movie treatment of different careers
- Hypermedia decision chart for vocational guidance
- Webliography on careers

Bibliography

Alliance for Technology Access. *Computer Resources for People with Disabilities.* Alameda, CA: Hunter House, 1994.

Anderson, M. A. *Teaching Information Literacy Using Electronic Resources, for Grades 6-12.* Worthington, OH: Linworth Publishing, 1996.

Armstrong, T. *Multiple Intelligences in the Classroom.* Alexandria, VA: Association for Supervision and Curriculum Development, 1994.

Barron, Ann E. *Getting Started with Telecommunications.* Tampa, FL: Florida Center for Instructional Technology, 1995.

Barron, Ann E. and K. S. Ivers. *The Internet and Instruction: Ideas and Activities.* Englewood, CO: Libraries Unlimited, 1996.

Barron, Ann E. and G. W. Orwig. *Multimedia Technologies for Training: An Introduction.* Englewood, CO: Libraries Unlimited, 1995.

Barron, Ann E. and Gary W. Orwig. *New Technologies for Education: A Beginner's Guide.* 3rd ed. Englewood, CO: Libraries Unlimited, 1997.

Baule, Steven M. *Technology Planning.* Worthington, OH: Linworth Publishing, 1997.

Bazeli, Marilyn J. *Technology Across the Curriculum: Activities and Ideas.* Englewood, CO: Libraries Unlimited, 1997.

Berge, Zane and Mauri Collins. *Wired Together: The Online Classroom in K-12.* 4 vol. San Jose, CA: Hampton, 1997.

Berger, Arthur Asa. *Media Research Techniques.* Thousand Oaks, CA: Sage Publications, 1998.

Bielefield, Arlene and Lawrence Cheeseman. *Technology and Copyright Law.* New York, NY: Neal-Schuman, 1997.

Big6 Newsletter.

Breivick, P. S. and J. A. Senn. *Information Literacy: Educating Children for the 21st Century.* New York, NY: Scholastic, 1994.

Brock, P. *Educational Technology in the Classroom.* Englewood Cliffs, NJ: Educational Technology Publications, 1994.

Brooks, J. G. and M. g. Brooks. *In Search of Understanding: The Case for Constructivist Classrooms.* Alexandria, VA: Association for Supervision and Curriculum Development, 1993.

Cable in the Classroom.

California Education Technology Task Force. *Connect, Compute, Compete.* Sacramento, CA: California Department of Education, 1996.

Bibliography continued

California Department of Education. *Caught in the Middle: Educational Reform for Young Adolescents in California Public Schools.* Sacramento, CA, 1987.

California Department of Education. *Second to None: A Vision of the California High School.* Sacramento, CA: California Department of Education, 1992.

California Media and Library Educators Association. *From Literacy Skills to Information Literacy: A Handbook for the 21st Century.* Castle Rock, CO: HiWillow, 1994.

California School Library Association. *Information Literate in Any Language.* Castle Rock, CO: HiWillow, 1995.

Casey, Jean M. *Early Literacy: The Empowerment of Technology.* Englewood, CO: Libraries Unlimited, 1997.

Castorina, C. ed. *Equal Access: Information Technology for Students with Disabilities.* New York, NY: McGraw-Hill, 1994.

Center for Media Literacy. www.media.lit.org/~cml.

Computing Teacher.

Conte, Christopher. *The Learning Connection: Schools in the Information Age.* Washington, DC: Benton Foundation, 1997.

Cooper, J. David. *Literacy: Helping Children Construct Meaning.* New York, NY: Houghton Mifflin, 1993.

Costa, Arthur L. *Supporting the Spirit of Learning: When Process is Content.* Thousand Oaks, CA: Corwin Press, 1997.

Craver, Kathleen. *Teaching Electronic Literacy: A Concepts-Based Approach for School Library Media Specialists.* Westport, CT: Greenwood, 1997.

Cummins, Jim, and Dennis Sayers. *Brave New Schools: Challenging Cultural Illiteracy Through Global Learning Networks.* New York, NY: St. Martin's Press, 1995.

Curchy, Christopher and Keith Kyker. *Educator's Survival Guide to TV Production, Equipment and Setup.* Englewood, CO: Libraries Unlimited, 1997.

Derich, Barbara, coordinator. *Technology Planning Guide for Curriculum Integration.* Larkspur, CA: Education Task Force, 1996.

Dertouzos, Michael I. *What Will Be: How the New World of Information Will Change Our Lives.* San Francisco, CA: Harper, 1997.

D'Ignazio, Fred. "An Inquiry-Centered Classroom of the Future." *The Classroom Teacher.* (March 1990) 16-19.

Doyle, Christina S. *Information Literacy in an Information Society: A Concept for the Information Age.* Syracuse, NY: ERIC Clearinghouse on Information & Technology, 1994.

Education Technology News.

Bibliography continued

Eisenberg, M. B. and R. E. Berkowitz. *Information Problem Solving: The Big Six Skills Approach Library and Information Skills Instruction.* Norwood, NJ: Ablex, 1990.

Eisenberg, M. B. and D. Johnson. *Computer Skills for Information Problem-Solving: Learning and Teaching Technology in Context.* Syracuse, NY: ERIC Clearinghouse on Information and Technology, 1996.

Electronic Learning.

Electronic School.

Ellsworth, J. H. *Education on the Internet: A Hands-on Book of Ideas, Resources, Projects, and Advice.* Indianapolis, IN: Sams Publishing, 1994.

Farmer, Lesley S. J. *Cooperative Learning Activities in the Library Media Center.* Rev. ed. Englewood, CO: Libraries Unlimited, 1998.

Farmer, Lesley S. J. *Creative Partnerships: Librarians and Teachers Working Together.* Worthingon, OH: Linworth Publishing, 1993.

Farmer, Lesley S. J. *Informing Young Women: Gender Equity through Literacy Skills.* Jefferson, NC: McFarland & Company, 1996.

From Now On: The Educational Technology Journal.

Garrett, Linda J. and JoAnne Moore. *Teaching Library Skills in Middle and High School.* Englewood, CO: Libraries Unlimited, 1993.

Gilster, Paul. *Digital Literacy.* New York, NY: John Wiley & Sons, 1997.

Gooden, A. *Computers in the Classroom: How Teachers and Students are Using Technology to Transform Learning.* San Francisco, CA: Jossey-Bass, 1996.

Harson, Charles. *Using the Internet, Online Services, and CD-ROMs for Writing Research and Term Papers.* New York, NY: Neal-Schuman, 1996.

Hirsch, E. D. *Cultural Literacy: What Every American Needs to Know.* New York, NY: Vintage, 1988.

Institute for Learning Technologies. www.ilt.columbia.edu.

Interactive Educational Systems Design. *Report of the Effectiveness of Technology in Schools.* Washington, DC: Software Publishers Association, 1994.

Ivers, Karen S. and Ann E. Barron. *Multimedia Projects in Education.* Englewood, CO: Libraries Unlimited, 1997.

Jay, M. Ellen and Hilda L. Jay. *The Library/Computer Lab/Classroom Connection.* New York, NY: Neal-Schuman, 1994.

Johnson, Steven. *Interface Culture: How New Technology Transforms the Way We Create and Communicate.* San Francisco, CA: Harper, 1997.

Bibliography continued

Jones, Debra. *Exploring the Internet Using Critical Thinking Skills.* New York, NY: Neal-Schuman, 1998.

Kemp, Jerrold E. and Don c. Smellie. *Planning, Producing, and Using Instructional Media.* 6th ed. New York, NY: Harper & Row, 1989.

Kolb, D. *Study and Information Skills Across the Curriculum.* London: Heinemann, 1995.

Langhorne, Mary Jo, ed. *Developing an Information Literacy Program K-12.* New York, NY: Neal-Schuman, 1998.

Lasarenko, J. *Wired for Learning.* Indianapolis, IN: Que Corporation, 1997.

Learning & Leading with Technology.

Lewis, Patrick. *Information Superhighway Bicycle Training Course.* New York, NY: Neal-Schuman, 1998.

Lewis, Patrick. *Information Superhighway Driver Training Course.* New York, NY: Neal-Schuman, 1997.

Magee, Mary. "Media Literacy: The New Basic." *Emergency Librarian.* 25:2 (Nov., 1997) 23-26.

Male, Mary. *Technology for Inclusion: Meeting the Special Needs of all Students.* Boston, MA: Allyn & Bacon, 1994.

Martin, Elizabeth M., ed. *The Challenge of Internet Literacy: The Instruction-Web Convergence.* Binghamton, NY: Haworth Press, 1997.

Maze, Susan and others. *Authoritative Guide to Web Search Engines.* New York, NY: Neal-Schuman, 1997.

McCain, Charles H. *Plugged In and Turned On: Planning, Coordinating, and Managing Computer-Supported Instruction.* Thousand Oaks, CA: Corwin Press, 1996.

McKenzie, Jamie. *Power Learning.* Newbury Park, CA: Corwin Press, 1993.

Media and Methods.

Media Awareness Network. www.screen.com/mnet/eng.

Mendrinos, Roxanne. *Building Information Literacy Using High Technology: A Guide for Schools and Libraries.* Englewood, CO: Libraries Unlimited, 1994.

Mid-Continent Regional Educational Laboratory. www.mcrel.org.

Multimedia World.

Multimedia Schools.

National Academy of Science. *Reinventing School: The Technology is Now.* Washington, DC: National Academy of Science, 1995.

Bibliography continued

National Information Center for Educational Media. nicem.com.

NewMedia.

Negroponte, Nicholaus. *Being Digital.* New York, NY: Knopf, 1995.

North Central Regional Educational Laboratory. www.ncrel.org.

North West Educational Technology Consortium. www.nwet.org.

Office of Technology Assessment. *Teachers and Technology: Making the Connection.* Washington, DC: U. S. Congress, 1995.

Papert, Seymour. *The Children's Machine: Rethinking School in the Age of the Computer.* New York, NY: Basic Books, 1993.

Perelman, J. J. *School's Out: Hyperlearning, the New Technology, and the End of Education.* New York, NY: William Morrow, 1992.

Perrone, V., ed. *Expanding Student Assessment.* Alexandria, VA: Association for Supervision and Curriculum Development, 1991.

Potter, W. James. *Media Literacy.* Thousand Oaks, CA: Sage Publications, 1998.

Pressley, Michael and Christine McCormick. *Cognition, Teaching and Assessment.* Reading, MA: Addison-Wesley, 1995.

Ramirez, R. and R. Bell. *Byting Back: Policies to Support the use of Technology in Education.* Oak Brook, IL: North Central Regional Educational Laboratory, 1994.

Real, Michael R. *Exploring Media Culture.* Thousand Oaks, CA: Sage Publications, 1996.

Roerden, L. *Net Lessons: Web-Based Projects for Your Classroom.* Sebastopol, CA: Songline Studios, Inc. and O'Reilly & Associates, 1996.

Routman, Regie. *Literacy at the Crossroads.* London: Heinemann, 1996.

Scrogan, L. *Tools for Change: Restructuring Technology in our Schools.* Boulder, CO: Institute for Effective Educational Practice, 1993.

Selfe, C. L., and S. Hilligoss, ed. *Literacy and Computers: The Complications of Teaching and Learning with Technology.* New York, NY: Modern Language Association, 1994.

Serim, F. and M. Koch. *Netlearning: Why Teachers Use the Internet.* Sebastopol, CA: Songline Studios, Inc. and O'Reilly & Associates, 1996.

Simpson, Carol and Sharron McEleel. *Copyright for Schools.* 2d ed. Worthington, OH: Linworth Publishing, 1997.

Sizer, Theodore. *Horace's Hope: What Works for the American High School.* Boston, MA: Houghton-Mifflin, 1996.

Stripling, Barbara K. *Libraries for the National Education Goals.* Syracuse, NY: ERIC Clearinghouse on Information Resources, 1992.

Bibliography continued

Syllabus.

Technology and Learning.

Technology Connection.

Technology for Diverse Learners. West Haven, CT: National Education Association, 1997.

T.H.E. Journal.

Umbach, Kenneth W. *Computer Technology in California K-12 Schools: Uses, Best Practices, and Policy Implications.* Sacramento, CA: California State Library, 1998.

U. S. Department of Labor. Secretary's Commission on Achieving Necessary Skills. *What Work Requires of Schools. A SCANS Report for America 2000.* Washington, DC: U. S. Government Printing Office, 1991.

Valauskas, Edward J. and Monica Ertel. *The Internet for Teachers and School Library Media Specialists.* New York, NY: Neal-Schuman, 1996.

Wilson, Brent G., ed. *Constructivist Learning Environments: Case Studies in Instructional Design.* Phoenix, AZ: Oryx Press, 1996.

Winn, P. G. *Integration of the Secondary School Library Media Center into the Curriculum.* Englewood, CO: Libraries Unlimited. 1991.

Worsnop, Chris M. *Assessing Media Work.* Mississauga, Canada: Wright Communications, 1996.

Wright, Kieth. *The Challenge of Technology: Action Strategies for the School Library Media Specialist.* Chicago, IL: American Library Association, 1993.

Index

AASL 42
Acceptable use policy 24
Administrators 24
Analog 10, 65
Annenberg 43
Assessment 12, 38, 40, 53, 70
Audio-visuals
   See multimedia
Benchmark 58-59
Bibliography 78
Books 5, 6, 13-16, 50
California 20-27, 59, 61-64
CD-ROM 71, 76
Classroom 12-13, 16-17
Collection 21-22
Computers 6, 10, 46-47, 50, 85-87
   See also technology
Constructivist 49, 52
Cooperative learning 38, 45-46, 63, 67
Copyright 71-78
Curriculum 52
Cycle of inquiry 60
Dertouzos 1-2
Descriptor 58
Design brief 87
Donation 24
E-mail 1, 86
Equipment 26-27, 69, 84
Evaluation 6
   See also assessment
Facilities 3, 9-17, 25, 30, 39, 67-68
Files 85-86
Filters 3, 6, 24
Fowler 59
Furniture 25
Hardware
   see equipment
Heat 25
Hirsch 41
Home 14, 67
Homework 50
Hypermedia 1, 26, 59, 70, 76

Indicator 58, 61-62
Information literacy 7, 38, 41-47, 52
Infrastructure 27-28
Inquiry 14, 71
Instruction 9-10, 12, 39, 45, 49, 51-52, 65
Internet 11-12, 22, 24, 31, 47, 71, 78, 84, 86
Jpeg 59
Kozol 83
LAN 14
Library media center 14, 22, 36-37, 52, 67
Library teacher 3, 7, 14, 25, 36
Literature review 84
Maintenance 22-25, 69
Mass media 43
Media 19-20
Media literacy 43-44
Megee 43
Multimedia 11-12, 14, 25, 53, 57, 65-72
Multiple intelligences 45
Music 86-87
Networks 11-12, 50-51
   See also LAN
Neuron 19
Outcomes 58-61
   See also standards
Parents 24
Partners 14, 35-36
Patent 78
Performance 49-53, 58
Planning 14, 37-40, 67-68
Policies 24
Portfolio 13, 58, 63, 71
Pre-requisite skills 38
Product 67
Program language 78
Reading 25, 41
Repurposing 75-76
Resources 19-30, 38-39, 46
Rubrics 2, 58
SCANS Report 63
Scheduling 17, 68
SCORE 22

Index continued

Search engine 22
Security 25
Selection 22
Sizer 41
Society 44
Software 14, 24, 26, 78
Standards 27-30, 53-58, 60
   See also assessment
Storyboard 17
Students 6-7, 12, 35, 38, 44-45, 47, 60, 65, 67
Supervision 25
Tamalpais Union High School District 58
Teacher 14, 19-21, 24-25, 29-30, 36-37, 47, 49-51, 53, 65, 67, 84-85
Technical literacy 30
Technicians 29, 36-37, 52, 67, 69
Technology 1-3, 24-25, 46-47, 52, 59, 61-62, 68
   See also computers
Telecommunications 27
Television 43, 85
Textbook 10, 12, 22, 52, 85-87
Training 20-21, 85
URL 31, 79
Video 4, 25, 76, 79, 87
Virus 69
WAN 13
Webliography 79-81
Word processing 47, 86
World War II 11

Lessons:
Animation 100-101, 112
Archetype 104
Architecture 96-97
Artist 106-107
Assessment 93, 95, 97, 99, 101, 103, 105, 107, 109, 111, 113
CAD 92, 96, 98
CD-ROM 97, 106-107
Chemistry 108

Content analysis 95-96
Cooperative learning 95
Economics 78
Energy 111
Food 112-113
Graphs 110-111
History 94-95, 102
Hypermedia 71, 108-109, 112-113
Internet 94, 96, 100, 109
Islam 94-95
Maps 93
Mathematics 98-99
Medieval 96
Morphing 106-107
Photography 107
Religion 94-95
Rome 92
Science 108-109
Storyboard 100
Three-D 97
Video 104-105
Water 110
Web 94, 102

www.ingramcontent.com/pod-product-compliance
Lightning Source LLC
Chambersburg PA
CBHW080541300426
44111CB00017B/2826